90

JN

D0753626

Sir Edmund Hillary

THE WORLD'S GREAT EXPLORERS

Edmund Hillary

By Timothy R. Gaffney

Consultant: Jeanne-Marie Gilbert
Consulting Editor
American Alpine Club Books

CHILDRENS PRESS ®

CHICAGO

Edmund Hillary, Tenzing Norgay, and two companions inching up toward Mount Everest's crest

Dedication: To Christine

Project Editor: Ann Heinrichs
Designer: Lindaanne Donohoe
Typesetter: Compositors Corporation
Engraver: Liberty Photoengraving

**Library of Congress
Cataloging-in-Publication Data**
Gaffney, Timothy R.
  Edmund Hillary : first to climb Mt. Everest / by Timothy R. Gaffney.
    p.   cm.—(The World's great explorers)
  Includes bibliographical references.
  Summary: A biography of Edmund Hillary, whose love of snow, mountains, and the outdoor life, culminated in his conquering the highest peak in the world.
  ISBN 0-516-03052-3
  1. Hillary, Edmund, Sir—Juvenile literature. 2. Mountaineers—Great Britain—Biography—Juvenile literature. 3. Mountaineering—Everest, Mount (China and Nepal)—Juvenile literature. 4. Everest, Mount (China and Nepal)—Description and travel—Juvenile literature. [1. Hillary, Edmund, Sir. 2. Mountaineers.]
  I. Title.   II. Series.
GV199.92.H54G34   1990
796.5′22′092—dc20
[B]   89-28624
                                     CIP
                                      AC

Sir John Hunt (left) and Sir Edmund Hillary in July 1953 after being knighted by Queen Elizabeth

Table of Contents

Chapter 1
Success!

C amp Four was a cold and primitive place. It was a cluster of tents 21,000 feet (6,400 meters) above sea level in the Himalayan Mountains. But on May 30, 1953, it was crowded. Most members of the British Mount Everest expedition had gathered there, waiting for news from the world's highest peak.

The camp radio was not working. The crowd knew nothing about the pair of climbers who had set out the day before from a tiny, lonely tent at 27,900 feet (8,504 meters). Had the pair reached the summit, 29,028 feet (8,848 meters) above sea level? Were they still alive?

Mount Everest is a steep, barren, windblown peak of rock and ice. The weather changes constantly, but the mountain is always dangerous. It rises so far into the sky that, at its upper reaches, the air is too thin to breathe safely. The climbers had to wear oxygen masks like jet pilots and carry small tanks of pressurized oxygen on their backs.

It was the expedition's second attempt to reach the summit. A different pair had tried on May 26. They had turned back short of their goal, so worn out that one had collapsed and had to be carried down the mountain. Everyone at Camp Four waited anxiously for a sign that would tell the fate of the latest pair.

A string of tiny dots appeared on a sweeping expanse of snow high above. The people at Camp Four counted the dots. There were five. Five dots meant that everybody—the two summit climbers and three others who had waited for them in another high camp—was still alive. On Everest, that was important news.

Still the people waited, wondering. Had the summit been reached? It was hard to follow the dots across the jumbled, icy landscape. The dots disappeared for a while. Then someone gave a shout. The climbers were coming out of a gully not far away. Camp Four emptied as everyone rushed toward the climbers. Suddenly, one of them raised an arm in a thumbs-up gesture. Everybody understood what that signal meant: Success!

The crowd reached the climbers at a run. Everyone began shouting, hugging, crying, and congratulating.

The celebrating continued long after everyone got back to Camp Four. But one member of the happy throng did not stay. James Morris, a reporter for *The Times* of London, scrambled down the mountain to get the story to his newspaper. Word would spread quickly; unless he hurried, another newspaper would get the story first.

When Morris reached the expedition's base camp far below Camp Four, he sent a runner to an Indian radio post with a message. It read: "Snow conditions bad stop Advanced base abandoned yesterday stop Awaiting improvement."

Hillary just after his historic climb of Mount Everest

The message leaked to other newspapers, and they hurried to publish it. But Morris had tricked them. It was a coded message for his editors at the *Times*. This is what it said to them:

Summit of Everest reached on 29 May
by Hillary and Tenzing.

Edmund Hillary, a beekeeper from New Zealand, and Tenzing Norgay, a Sherpa from Nepal, had reached the highest point on earth.

Chapter 2
The Beekeeper
Climbs the Alps

Edmund Hillary was born in Auckland, New Zealand, on July 20, 1919. New Zealand lies about 1,250 miles (2,012 kilometers) southeast of Australia in the South Pacific Ocean. Its domain includes two large islands and a number of small ones. The two main islands are known simply as North Island and South Island. Between them lies Cook Strait, which separates the islands by as little as 16 miles (26 kilometers) at its narrowest point.

Both islands have mountain ranges. On South Island, running like a spine along the west coast, is a range called the Southern Alps. Its highest peak is Mount Cook, 12,349 feet (3,764 meters). North Island is mountainous in its central and southern areas. Its highest peak is Mount Ruapehu, standing 9,175 feet (2,797 meters) high near the center of the island.

Hillary was born on North Island, though not in the mountains. He grew up in dairy country to the north, surrounded by gentle hills and pastures. He would be close to adulthood before the mountains first cast their spell on him.

The Hillary family lived in a roomy house on a small farm about 40 miles (65 kilometers) south of Auckland. Ed had an older sister and a younger brother. His father edited and published a weekly newspaper until he started a family honey business. The Hillarys worked hard, tending beehives and gathering honey. Holidays, vacations, and even spending money were rare.

Ed grew from a small and scrawny child to a tall, lean teenager. He finished elementary school at age eleven, two years ahead of schedule. Then he rode a train to Auckland every day for three years to attend high school. Ed was quiet and found it hard to mix with the other students, but he devoured adventure stories, sometimes reading a book a day. In his mind he became a great explorer.

Young Hillary got his first taste of adventure in 1935 at the age of sixteen. With a group of school friends, he went on a ten-day ski trip to Mount Ruapehu. High above sea level, where the air was cooler, he saw snow for the first time in his life. He skied, got into snowball fights, and built snowmen. He had little interest in climbing to the top of Ruapehu, but he fell in love with the snow.

After high school, Ed attended a university. However, he was more interested in the family beekeeping business. After two years he quit school to help take care of the family's 1,600 beehives. It was hard work, but he enjoyed the sun and fresh air.

Soon, however, his love for the outdoor life drew him back to the mountains. During late 1939 and early 1940, he took a trip with some friends to the Southern Alps on New Zealand's South Island. This time of year is winter in the Northern Hemisphere but summer in the Southern Hemisphere, where Australia and New

New Zealand's Mount Ruapehu, its snowy peak rising in contrast to the tropical vegetation below

Zealand are. One evening as he relaxed in a lounge, he noticed two men who seemed to be the center of attention. These were real mountain climbers, the first Hillary had ever seen. They had just returned from climbing Mount Cook.

The next morning, Hillary and a friend hired a mountain guide. Before reaching the top of a mountain, they stopped on an airy ridge, but Hillary had to go on. Alone, he scrambled up to the rocky summit, where the air was brisk and clear. Hillary felt as if he were standing on the top of the world.

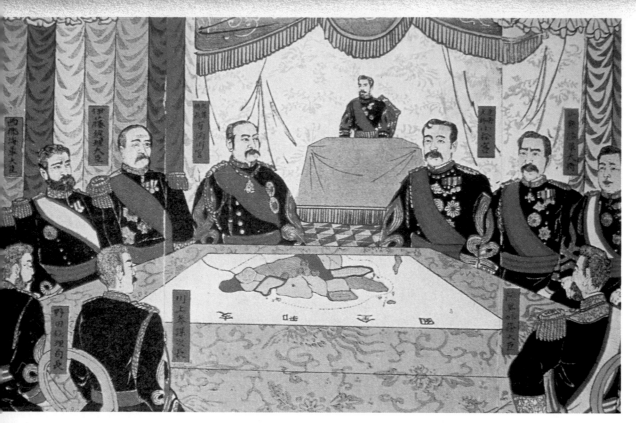

Japanese generals of the Meiji period (1867-1912). During this time, Japan greatly expanded the borders of its empire and began its rise as an industrial power.

The world was changing during these times, however. To the north, Japan was spreading its military might into Asia and across the Pacific Ocean. In Europe, Nazi German troops were storming across the continent. Their invasions started World War II.

Hillary wanted to join the New Zealand Air Force and learn to fly. At the same time, he had a strong Christian belief that it was wrong to kill other people. Neither was he required to join the military. New Zealand considered farmers to be essential and did not force them to serve. After a period of indecision, he applied to the air force in 1942. Early in 1944, he was called to duty.

Hillary's training camp was located in a mountain valley. Naturally, he spent his free time exploring the mountains. While the other airmen went into town, Hillary tramped up and down the ridges. For Hillary, preparing for war was like a holiday.

By this time he was six feet, two inches (188 centimeters) tall and weighed 190 pounds (86 kilograms). He was also an experienced wilderness traveler. On a ten-day Christmas holiday in 1944, he decided to try New Zealand's most challenging peak, Mount Cook.

He thought twice, however, when he saw Mount Cook's steep, glacier-covered slopes. They presented a serious danger of avalanches and crevasses. An avalanche, a great mass of sliding snow, can sweep down and bury a climber in seconds. A crevasse is a deep crack that may lie hidden under the snow like a deadly trap. Hillary had no climbing partner, and he knew it would be foolish to tackle Mount Cook alone. Instead, he settled for more modest peaks.

In the air force, Hillary was trained as a navigator and sent to the Solomon Islands in the South Pacific. Earlier in the war, U.S. Marines had reclaimed the islands from the Japanese. Thus Hillary would not have to fly any combat missions. Instead he went on search and rescue missions, and in his spare time he read books about great adventures. He found a book on the Himalayan Mountains of Nepal and read it eagerly.

A glacier's crevasse, partially hidden beneath the snow

Japan's surrender ended the war in August 1945. While many of New Zealand's forces were called home, Hillary's unit was kept on standby for rescue missions. The men had to stay close to base, so they amused themselves by rebuilding an old motorboat they had found.

The motorboat was fast and fun to drive. But one morning its fuel tank caught fire, and Hillary and a friend suffered serious burns. Hillary lost 40 percent of his skin, a grave injury. He was rushed to a U.S. military hospital on Guadalcanal, an island in the Solomon group, where he recovered quickly. After only three weeks of treatment, he was able to return to duty.

Hillary and mountain guide Harry Ayres study the Tasman Glacier near Mount Cook, hoping to find a suitable training area for their climbing expedition.

The New Zealand Air Force soon sent him back to Auckland, where he returned to civilian life. Back home, he immersed himself once again in the family beekeeping business and spent his leisure time trekking through New Zealand's mountains. But that leisure activity was about to take up more and more of his time.

In the summer of 1947, Hillary became friends with a well-known New Zealand mountain guide, Harry Ayres. They met in a mountain hut and began climbing together.

Ayres was the skilled partner Hillary felt he needed to tackle Mount Cook. They got an early start, setting off at 1:00 one morning under a cold, clear sky. Travel was slow in the early-morning darkness as they made their way through blocks of ice and fields full of crevasses. The top of the mountain was cloaked in ice, but they reached it. From there Hillary gazed in wonder at the mountain's lower peaks beneath him. It was a wonderful moment and a big step in his climbing career.

Over the next few years, Ayres was Hillary's frequent climbing companion on New Zealand mountains. Ayres was careful, but not fearful—and their climbs had plenty of hair-raising moments.

Aerial view of a valley in the Austrian Alps, where Hillary scaled several peaks after climbing Mount Cook.

Soon Hillary had a chance to try some of Europe's famous peaks. His sister was studying in England and was planning to be married there. Hillary and his brother bought the family bee business, which enabled his parents to travel to England to see their daughter. Hillary later joined them on their tour of Europe.

Of course, Hillary included climbing in his plans. He had brought his climbing boots and ice axe halfway around the world with him. After his family tour, he joined two friends from New Zealand for adventure in the Alps of Austria and Switzerland. Mountain climbing, or mountaineering, was an old and popular pastime in the Alps. For a small fee, Hillary and his friends could stay in comfortable huts in the mountains, where cooks prepared hearty meals. However, they did not want to hire guides, as most European climbers did.

The lofty Matterhorn, a peak in the Swiss Alps

They climbed several peaks in Austria, then rode a train to Switzerland. The Swiss Alps offered some of the world's best mountain climbing. Its great peaks include the Matterhorn and the Eiger. Railroads wound around and even through the mountains. Many climbers began their ascents from the scenic mountain railway tunnels.

Hillary and his friends decided to launch their first climb from a railway tunnel to a peak named Jungfrau. The route they planned to take was no longer being used, and the train conductor warned them not to try it. They found out why at the hut where they had planned to stay that night: The hut was empty. There was no one there to cook their food—and for that matter, there was no food. They went to bed hungry, but the next day they climbed anyway, reaching the 13,642-foot (4,158-meter) summit of Jungfrau.

Alpine railway, with Jungfrau rising in the background. Jungfrau's mountain railway, terminating at 4,406 feet (1,334 meters), is the highest rail ascent in Europe.

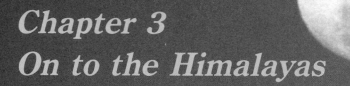

Chapter 3
On to the Himalayas

For many climbers, one mountain range stands out as the goal of a lifetime: the Himalayas. The Himalayan Mountains spread in a great mass across India, Nepal, and China. On the highest peaks, the air is too thin for most people to breathe. Glaciers creep in frozen rivers around the peaks, sometimes forming steep drops, or icefalls. Icefalls are unstable, and blocks of ice called seracs, bigger than houses, can tumble down them at any time.

Frostbite is another threat. A climber's feet can easily grow numb, then freeze on the surface. Frostbite can cripple, too. When severely frostbitten, a climber's toes or feet may have to be amputated. Even so, climbers are drawn to the Himalayas because of their fabulous beauty and because they offer the world's greatest climbing challenges.

Hillary was thinking of the Himalayas in 1950, even before he finished his European climbing trip. Other New Zealand climbers were planning a Himalayan expedition—the first by New Zealanders—and they invited Hillary to join them. They included George Lowe, a schoolteacher and an excellent climber; Earle Riddiford, a young attorney; and Ed Cotter. They would need a lot of climbing equipment, and they would have to pay for it out of their pockets. That did not discourage Hillary.

Their goal was to climb Mukut Parbat, a 23,760-foot (7,242-meter) peak in India just west of Nepal. They prepared by climbing some New Zealand peaks together early in 1951. It was important to find out how well they could work together. They knew that four excellent climbers who did not get along would not make a good team. They were pleased to find that they all got along well.

The four climbers set out on their adventure in May 1951. First they flew to Australia, and from there they sailed west to India. Leaving the modern world farther behind all the time, they rode trains across the flat country toward the mountains.

A bus took them to the foot of the Himalayas at the town of Ranikhet. There they had arranged to meet four Sherpas from Nepal who would serve as porters and guides. Hillary had read about the hardy Sherpa people who live in small villages high in the Himalayas. He found the Sherpas he met were rugged, and also friendly and cheerful. He liked them immediately.

After hiring thirty more local people as porters, they made a 100-mile (161-kilometer) trek to the village of Badrinath. From there they set out for their introduction to Himalayan climbing.

Before attempting Mukut Parbat, they climbed a tall spire called Nilcanta, whose summit reaches 21,600 feet (6,584 meters). The air grew thinner the higher they went. Steps had to be cut in the steep ice slopes so the climbers could get a foothold on the sheer mountain face. Plunging through wet snow and cutting steps exhausted them. They retreated from Nilcanta without reaching its summit, then tried an unnamed peak nearby. (With so many peaks in the area, many of them had no name.) Again they were forced to retreat.

They rested in Badrinath, then trekked up a river gorge and across glaciers to Mukut Parbat. At 16,000 feet (4,877 meters), they made a base camp—Camp One—and left most of their supplies there. Above the base camp they pitched a series of higher camps, each one a day's climb above the last.

Schoolteacher and mountaineer George Lowe (right) accompanied Hillary on several expeditions, including one to Antarctica, which the two are shown discussing here.

Mukut Parbat offered no easy route to its summit. Steep ice cliffs threatened to drop great chunks of ice on the climbers. The air grew ever thinner and colder. Frostbite was a constant threat—their feet were always cold and could easily grow numb.

The climbers made Camp Three at 21,000 feet (64,000 meters). The next day at dawn, they started out for the summit. As in all serious mountaineering, the climbers were attached to each other by ropes for safety. Riddiford, Cotter, and a Sherpa named Passang made up one rope team; Hillary and Lowe formed the other.

Hillary and Lowe led at first, but their feet were bitterly cold. They stopped to warm them while the other team pushed ahead. Riddiford's team reached the summit after a long day, but Hillary and Lowe retreated back to Camp Three. Hillary was disappointed that he had not reached the summit, but he admired the willpower Riddiford had used to keep going.

They retraced their route back to Badrinath and rested for several days. Hillary and Lowe were not about to quit without conquering at least one peak. There was still some equipment left in the high camps. With some Sherpas, they returned to Camp Three. From there they climbed a 22,180-foot (6,760-meter) peak before bad weather finally drove them away.

The New Zealanders left the mountains on August 14, 1951. After three months, their adventure was over—or so they thought.

Back in Ranikhet, they found a telegram from famous British explorer Eric Shipton. His books about Himalayan adventures had fired Hillary's interest in the mountains. Now Shipton planned to scout new routes up Mount Everest, and he was inviting two men from Hillary's group to join him.

Foothills of the Himalayas

A medieval trail from Tibet to India snakes its way around a Himalayan mountainside.

Who would go? Hillary was in top shape and an obvious choice; Riddiford and Lowe were both good climbers, but Riddiford had more money to pay for his expenses. With the Sherpas Passang and Nima, Hillary and Riddiford raced to catch up with Shipton in the kingdom of Nepal.

Nepal is a small, rectangular country bordered on three sides by India. To the north is Tibet, once an independent nation but now a part of China. Straddling the border between Nepal and Tibet is a barrier of high Himalayan peaks that includes Mount Everest.

Mountaineers Eric Shipton (left) and Tom Bourdillon (right) leaving London for India in August 1951 to begin scouting routes up Mount Everest

After four days, Hillary's group caught up with Shipton in the Nepalese village of Dingla. With Shipton were Bill Murray, a Scottish climber; Michael Ward, a physician; and Tom Bourdillon, a physicist. The monsoon season had brought drenching rains, making muddy trails and swollen streams to cross. But Hillary was excited. They would be exploring parts of Nepal that no Europeans had ever visited.

Before 1951, Nepal had kept its borders closed to outsiders. Expeditions to Mount Everest had to approach the peak from the north, across Tibet. Then in 1951, the communist People's Republic of China sent soldiers to occupy Tibet. This sealed off the northern approach to Everest. But Nepal opened its borders that same year. Expeditions then began exploring the region south of Everest to find new ways to reach it. That was the purpose of Shipton's expedition.

From Dingla the climbers hiked through rough, wild country for eleven days. Their destination was the Sherpa village of Namche Bazar, then and now the southern gateway to the Everest region.

Namche Bazar lies east of Kathmandu, the capital of Nepal, in Nepal's Solu-Khumbu region. Although Shipton followed a different route, later expeditions would form at Kathmandu. From there they would trek through river valleys to Namche Bazar, at a fork in the Dudh Kosi River.

From Namche Bazar, the route to Everest is northeast along the Dudh Kosi River to the Thyangboche Monastery. Roads now take tourists part of the way to Namche Bazar from Kathmandu, and short airstrips dot the way for people in a hurry. But in the early 1950s, the only way to reach Namche Bazar was on foot.

Sherpas of Namche Bazar

Thyangboche Monastery

Hillary found Thyangboche Monastery surrounded by incredible mountain scenery. The sky was clear. Massive peaks soared all around, sparkling with snow.

Ahead was the route to Everest. It would take them up the Khumbu Glacier to the Western Cwm (pronounced "coom"). A cwm is a steep valley enclosed by mountains. The Western Cwm was surrounded by three great peaks: Nuptse on the south (24,850 feet; 7,574 meters), Lhotse on the east (27,890 feet; 8,500 meters), and Everest on the north (29,028 feet; 8,848 meters). The walls of the Western Cwm were formed by sharp, windblown ridges connecting the peaks. At the foot of Lhotse, a jumble of ice and snow marks the start of the Khumbu Glacier. The Khumbu extends westward past Nuptse, then turns south in a steep, frozen drop called the Khumbu Icefall.

On September 29, 1951, the expedition reached a wall of ice. It was the foot of the Khumbu Glacier. The climbers headed north alongside the glacier, skirting the ice on grassy fields. They climbed onto hills overlooking the glacier to scout the route ahead.

The Khumbu Icefall was frightening to behold. A high-flying airplane had photographed the area in 1933. In 1950, an expedition had pushed partway up the Khumbu Glacier. Both times, observers had seen what Shipton's group now saw: a steep drop from the upper glacier that formed a wild icefall blocking their way to Everest. A steep jumble of ridges and crevasses loomed before them. House-size blocks of ice perched at the lip of ice cliffs, ready to crash without warning down the frozen slopes. The route looked treacherous, if not impossible. There was only one thing to do.

They headed up the middle of the icefall.

Khumbu Icefall

Glacial runoff on the Tibet side of Mount Everest

Earle Riddiford and Passang led the first attempt on September 30. The group climbed in pairs, fighting snowstorms for three days. On the fourth day, they were climbing above a gaping crevasse when the fresh, loose snow underfoot began to slide.

Shipton, Hillary, and Passang leaped to safety, but the avalanche carried Riddiford toward the abyss. He and Passang were on the same rope, and the avalanche threatened to drag Passang along with Riddiford. But Passang quickly anchored himself and belayed the rope, saving both of them. Belaying is a safety measure for stopping falls. The higher climber secures the rope to the mountainside using a chock, piton, or ice screw.

That brush with disaster convinced the climbers to retreat until the snow was more stable. Meanwhile, they explored the country around them. Splitting into two groups, they hiked over passes and into snow-filled valleys never seen by Europeans. Hillary went east with Shipton, while another group went west. This group looked for a way across a high pass called Nup La on the border of Tibet. Steep icefalls turned them back.

Hillary and Shipton returned on October 19 and climbed up the Khumbu Icefall. They went just far enough to see that they could reach the Western Cwm. At last Shipton found what he had set out to learn: The key to reaching Everest from the south was to climb the treacherous Khumbu Icefall.

All the members of the expedition met at the base camp on October 25. By then, Hillary and Riddiford had been in the Himalayas for six months. Worried about the family honey business, Hillary wanted to leave. Riddiford agreed to go with him. While the rest of the expedition continued, Hillary and Riddiford hiked back to Kathmandu.

Hillary felt happy and victorious. They had discovered a way to reach Everest from the south. He had also spent two months with Eric Shipton, one of the world's greatest explorers. But jolting news greeted him in Kathmandu: Nepal had granted a Swiss expedition permission to climb Everest in 1952.

Rani Pokhari ("Queen's Pond") in Kathmandu at sunset

Chapter 4
The Challenge of Everest

In 1852, British surveyors established that the top of Mount Everest was the highest point on earth. The peak was named after Sir George Everest, who at the time was serving as the surveyor-general of India. To local peoples, however, the mountain is better known as Chomolungma, meaning "Goddess Mother of the World."

Surrounded by craggy peaks, Everest for years seemed not only impossible to climb but impossible even to find. As British mountaineer Sir George Mallory said, "It would be necessary in the first place to find the mountain."

Everest became the ultimate challenge for serious climbers. In 1921 Mallory began leading a British expedition up the slopes of Everest, but lost his life in the attempt. Over the next three decades, many others tried. But deep snow, bitter cold, sheer rock and ice, vicious winds, and oxygen-thin air overcame even the most expert climbers. With each successive failure, the challenge of Everest became more like a race for the top.

Cho Oyu

In 1952, Great Britain's Royal Geographic Society and Alpine Club decided to sponsor yet another Everest expedition. Despite news of the Swiss attempt, they continued with their plans. They would mount an expedition in 1952 to train for the actual attempt a year later. For the training climb, they picked a good target: Cho Oyu, 26,750 feet (8,153 meters) high, was one of the world's ten highest peaks and only 30 miles (48 kilometers) west of Everest.

Shipton led again and invited Hillary to join his expedition. Hillary was glad to learn that his friends Riddiford and Lowe were also invited.

They met in Nepal on March 29, 1952, and trekked into the mountains. Approaching Cho Oyu from the south, they saw no way to reach the top. Hillary and

Lowe explored to the north and saw what they thought might be a way. The route, however, would require that they cross the border into forbidden Tibet.

They had heard that Chinese soldiers patrolled the border, but Hillary and Lowe decided to try anyway. They cut across the border but made no camps in Tibet. Next they hiked up a glacier, climbed a ridge on the north side of Cho Oyu, and set up a camp at 21,000 feet (6,400 meters), back inside Nepal.

The way to the summit was hazardous. There was a choice between ice cliffs or a steep ice slope overhung with jagged blocks of ice. The expedition reached only 22,500 feet (6,858 meters). Although Cho Oyu remained unconquered, Hillary and Lowe climbed four other peaks higher than 20,000 feet (6,096 meters).

After the group left Cho Oyu, Shipton sent Hillary and Lowe to scout a way across the Nup La Pass into the Everest region from the west. (A group on Shipton's last expedition had tried to cross Nup La Pass from the east side but had failed.) Hillary and Lowe set off with five Sherpas.

Mount Everest from the base camp on the Tibet side

They had to fight their way up an icefall. It took days of brutal effort, but finally they reached the top of the pass and could look across the West Rongbuk Glacier to the massive pyramid of Everest. They went over the pass and trekked around the north side of Everest, again trespassing into Tibet.

The spectacular views of Everest reaching into the sky, its summit streaming snow in fierce winds high above, made them eager for the next expedition, when they would attempt to climb the giant itself. But the Swiss expedition worried them. Its climbers were somewhere on the mountain. Would they reach the summit? Were they already there?

Hillary and Lowe rejoined Shipton in Pangboche, a village near Namche Bazar, on June 9. Shipton had news about the Swiss expedition: Raymond Lambert and a Sherpa had reached 28,000 feet (8,534 meters) on Everest, but no higher. The Swiss group failed in another attempt later in the year. The summit remained untouched.

Meanwhile, the Alpine Club was planning its Everest attempt. This time the club did not put Shipton in charge. Although Shipton was a bold explorer, the committee did not have confidence in his desire to conquer mountains. His expedition's failure to reach the top of Cho Oyu worked against him.

To the Alpine Club, the Everest expedition would be like a small army marching into battle. The club picked a military co-leader for Shipton, British army colonel Henry Cecil John Hunt. Shipton was offended and offered to quit. The club let him go, over the protests of several expedition members.

John Hunt was known as a strong leader, a remarkable organizer, and he was no stranger to mountains. Born in 1910, he had been climbing since the age of fifteen—over twenty-five years. By the time his name went before the Everest committee, he had been on five Himalayan expeditions.

Hunt planned to make three summit attempts over the same number of days. For this he needed ten primary climbers, supported by a larger number of Sherpas. He began naming climbers, and both Hillary and George Lowe were on his list.

The expedition formed at Kathmandu. The food and supplies needed for the expedition required so many porters that two groups were formed, one of 150 and one of 200. The first group left on March 10, 1953.

Henry Cecil John Hunt, leader of the British Mount Everest expedition

"Prayer wheels" inside Thyangboche Monastery

The second group left the next day. A resupply group followed the same path a month later.

The first major stop was the Thyangboche Monastery, sixteen days by foot from Kathmandu. The expedition camped in a yak field there for three weeks. Meanwhile, the climbers practiced on nearby peaks and let their bodies adjust to the high altitude and cold weather. This period of adjustment is called acclimatization.

On April 9, Hillary led five members of the main climbing party, five Sherpas, and thirty-nine porters up the Khumbu Glacier. They reached the foot of the dangerous Khumbu Icefall on April 12. They found the site of the old Swiss base camp and decided to locate their own Camp One in the same spot.

Yak herders' hut at 15,000 feet (4,572 meters) in the Everest region

Hillary led the exploration of the icefall. They had to find the least dangerous route, but no route could be called safe in that creeping maze of crevasses and seracs. It was all too common for the mountaineers to mark a path, only to come back later and find it buried under a huge block of ice.

They set up Camp Two on a shelf halfway up the icefall. The section above them looked even worse, but the next day they fought their way to the top. They set up Camp Three at 20,200 feet (6,157 meters)—almost 4 miles (6.4 kilometers) above sea level—on April 22.

On this expedition, Hillary and the Sherpa Tenzing Norgay met for the first time. Tenzing was strong and sturdy, and he impressed Hillary immediately. In his book *High Adventure,* Hillary wrote, "He had the quiet air of confidence that quickly picked him out from his fellow Sherpas."

Tenzing was not like most Sherpas who worked on the expedition. While he needed the money he made, he was a climber at heart. Reaching the summit of Everest had been his lifelong dream. In fact, he had more Everest experience than anyone else on this expedition. He had worked on the Swiss expedition and had been among the first to climb the Khumbu Icefall and enter the Western Cwm. Tenzing was the Sherpa who had reached 28,000 feet (8,534 meters) with Raymond Lambert on the Swiss expedition.

Hillary and Tenzing teamed up late in April. Both men were strong and eager to climb. They got along well together and quickly took the lead. Along the way they found remains of the Swiss advance camps, including food that had been left behind. Refrigerated by the glacier, the food was still edible. On April 26, they set up Camp Four at 21,000 feet (6,400 meters), at the foot of Lhotse.

Khumbu Glacier

Summit ridge of Lhotse

The expedition was planning to take a route up the west face of Lhotse, a 27,890-foot (8,500-meter) peak south of Everest. After climbing most of the way up the Lhotse face, they would turn north and cross to Everest's South Col. (A col is a dip in a ridge that connects mountain peaks.) From the col, they would follow the ridgeline up Everest to its south summit. This was easier than trying to go directly up the side of Everest itself.

Hillary and Tenzing did not stay in the lead. At high altitudes, the body slowly wears itself out, so climbers take turns leading. Hillary and Tenzing spent the early part of May at Camp One, below the Khumbu Icefall. They watched through binoculars as other climbers pushed the route up Lhotse.

Hillary was restless at the base camp, but important decisions were being made there. On May 7, Hunt called a meeting to announce who would be on the teams that would try to reach the summit. Out of all the hundreds in the expedition, only a few would actually have a chance to stand on the top of Everest.

First, Hunt outlined his plan for the summit attempts. The first team would leave from the South Col and climb the southeast ridge to Everest's south summit. The very top of Everest is the north summit. But only if the first team still felt good after reaching the south summit was it to try to press on to the higher one.

Meanwhile, another group would set up a high camp on the southeast ridge above the col. After climbing to the high camp, the second team would then strike out for the north summit. Because of the thin air, both teams would have to carry oxygen tanks.

Hunt decided that the first team, headed for the south summit, would include Tom Bourdillon and Charles Evans, the deputy leader. They would use experimental, lightweight oxygen breathing gear developed by Bourdillon, a physicist, and his scientist father.

The second team would use heavier but well-proven oxygen gear. Given good weather, the second team would have a better chance of reaching Mount Everest's true summit.

The two climbers on that team, Hunt announced, would be Hillary and Tenzing.

Chapter 5
On Top of the World

Hillary and Tenzing waited while other climbers struggled up the Lhotse face—4,000 feet (1,219 meters) of steep ice and snow slopes. At the bottom was a dangerous jumble of crevasses and seracs where the face gave way to glacier. Daily snows had blanketed the face with soft snow. That made climbing harder and increased the risk of avalanches. Still, the Lhotse face was the only possible route.

Hunt assigned George Lowe the task of leading the way up the face to the South Col with two team climbers and several Sherpas. But the team climbers fell ill and had to turn back, making progress slow. Wilfrid Noyce, a schoolteacher and writer, joined Lowe on May 15. They set up Camp Seven the next day at 24,000 feet (7,315 meters).

Dawn in the village of Louché, altitude 16,200 feet (4,938 meters), a settlement along the Everest route

By then it had been six days since Lowe had set out to reach the col. Faced with deep snow, brutally cold wind, and thin air, his group seemed unable to get much farther than Camp Seven. Time was running out: They were close to the monsoon season—a season that, in the Himalayas, brought heavy snowstorms. Hillary urged Hunt to send him and Tenzing up to help, but Hunt refused. He wanted them to save their strength.

Noyce came down for a rest on May 17, then went back up three days later to force the route to the col. Lowe came down, worn out after eleven days above 23,000 feet (7,010 meters).

The next day, Noyce set out again to reach the South Col. But Hunt was anxious because Noyce had made a late start. Giving in to Hillary's pleas, Hunt sent him and Tenzing up to Camp Seven. They were to go no farther unless it was absolutely necessary to help set up Camp Eight on the col. But, once unleashed, Hillary and Tenzing charged ahead.

They reached Camp Seven in time to greet Noyce when he returned from the col. Then they decided to help lead Sherpas with supplies up to the col the following day.

They found the South Col a frozen, lonely spot of stony rubble and patches of hard, blue ice.

"I have been in many wild and lonely places in my life," Tenzing later recalled, "but never anywhere like the South Col."

Eerily occupying the col were the ghosts of the Swiss expedition: tent poles standing forlornly, with shreds of canvas fluttering and snapping in the constant wind. On each side, the level ground dropped away thousands of feet to the glaciers. The col ended where the southeast ridge of Everest soared into the sky. The south summit towered more than half a mile (.8 kilometers) above them, trailing great plumes of wind-driven snow.

Hillary and Tenzing did not stay at Camp Eight, nor even at Camp Seven. They zoomed back down and reached Camp Four that evening. It was an amazing feat of high-altitude endurance, and Hunt worried that it had sapped the strength they needed to reach the summit.

Bourdillon and Evans set out for their summit assault on May 24. They reached the South Col and rested the next day while Hillary, Tenzing, and a support group moved into Camp Seven to prepare their own assault.

On May 26, Hillary and Tenzing headed for the South Col again. They could see climbers high above them on the southeast ridge. John Hunt and two Sherpas dropped off a load of supplies on the ridge and turned back. Bourdillon and Evans kept going. At 1:00 P.M., they climbed out of sight over the south summit. They were higher than any person had ever climbed.

Clouds soon moved in and hid them from view. Hillary could only wait to find out whether he had lost his chance to be first to the top.

At 3:30, Bourdillon and Evans climbed down out of the clouds, moving just a few weary steps at a time. Coated with ice, and with oxygen masks covering their faces, they looked like creatures from another planet. They had climbed to 28,700 feet (8,748 meters), but their efforts had exhausted them. Now less than 230 feet (70 meters) away, the summit was still unclaimed.

High winds prevented any climbing the next day. The following morning, May 28, was windy and cold, but the winds had dropped. Hillary, Tenzing, George Lowe, Alf Gregory, and Ang Nyima loaded up supplies for another camp. This one was to be on the southeast ridge at 27,350 feet (8,336 meters). That was where Hunt's team had dropped off their load of supplies. But when they reached it, they decided to try to make the camp a little higher. They picked up what Hunt's team had left and climbed on. Each person now carried more than 50 pounds (23 kilograms). Hillary was supposed to be saving his energy, but he was carrying over 60 pounds (27 kilograms). It was an incredible weight to carry at such high altitudes.

They were getting desperate to find a place suitable for a campsite when Lowe discovered a level spot. With great relief, they dropped their loads at 27,900 feet

West summit ridge of Lhotse, whose western face was used as an approach to Everest. Its summit, at 27,890 feet (8,500 meters), reaches roughly the same altitude as Camp Nine.

(8,504 meters). Lowe, Gregory, and Ang Nyima went wearily back down to Camp Eight on the col, while Hillary and Tenzing scratched out a tent site—Camp Nine—on the steep slope.

The morning of May 29 was cloudless and calm. The two climbers heated drinks and tested their breathing gear. Hillary's feet were cold and his boots were frozen. He thawed them over their little stove.

By 6:30 A.M. they were moving up the ridge. They found a pair of partially charged oxygen bottles that Bourdillon and Evans had left. That was good because they had no oxygen to spare. They left the bottles for their trip down.

After climbing a frightfully steep stretch of snow, they reached the south summit at 9:00 A.M. Ahead was the last ridge between them and the top of the world. It was a narrow, savage-looking route. Along its edge, snow was wind-molded into frozen, overhanging waves called cornices. The cornices hung out over the edge of the ridge with thousands of feet of empty space below. A cornice could break off underfoot or a climber could fall through. To the left, the ridge fell away steeply to the Western Cwm. The tents of Camp Four were tiny specks a mile and a half (2.5 kilometers) below.

Hillary led the way carefully, cutting steps and skirting the dangerous tops of the cornices. Tenzing followed, belaying him with the rope.

A mountaineer in the region of Mount Everest

An ice wall in the Everest region

After an hour, they came to one last barrier—a vertical, 40-foot (12-meter) rock cliff. Even in New Zealand, this cliff would have been tough. At this altitude and in their condition, it just looked impossible.

Hillary found a wide, vertical crack between the rock and a wall of ice. The ice wall was a snow cornice that had formed against the rock and hardened. He climbed into the crack and began worming his way up, his back to the ice. If his weight made the ice wall peel away, he would fall into open space. But the ice held. He worked his way to the top, then anchored the rope while Tenzing followed.

They continued upward, edging past one hump of corniced snow after another. The ridge curved to the right, and each new cornice blocked their view. They could not tell how much farther they had to go.

Above: Conquest of the peak
*Below: Ruins along an Everest route
on the Tibetan side*

At 11:30 A.M., Hillary rounded a cornice and found himself looking into Tibet. The ridge they had been climbing now fell steeply away to the North Col and the Rongbuk Glacier. To his right was a narrow ridge that led to a snow-covered crest. After chipping steps in the slope, the two climbed to the top.

Now the world fell away from them on all sides. They were on the summit of Everest—the roof of the world. They shook hands, then hugged.

For fifteen minutes they took pictures and dug holes in the snow to leave mementos. Hillary left a crucifix, which John Hunt had asked him to do. Tenzing, a Buddhist, left offerings of chocolate, candy, and biscuits for the gods thought to dwell on Everest.

They ate a snack for energy, then climbed down the way they had come. With victory behind them, they felt their strength draining away. They passed the south summit within an hour and reached Camp Nine at 2:00 P.M., where they stopped to rest and heat sweet tea. Then they hooked up their last oxygen bottles—those that Bourdillon and Evans had left. They tied their sleeping bags onto their packs and headed down again.

George Lowe met them just above the South Col and poured mugs of hot soup from an insulated bottle. They told him of their victory, but they were too tired to show much enthusiasm.

Soon Hillary and Tenzing were burrowed into their sleeping bags on the South Col, bone-tired and cold but unable to sleep well. The next day, still weak, they moved slowly across the Lhotse face, stopping for hot drinks at Camp Seven. Then they headed down the face to the crowd waiting at Camp Four.

Exhilarated and exhausted, Hillary and Tenzing flash smiles after their Everest ascent.

Chapter 6
Exploring the Barun Valley

Hillary, with his guide Tenzing, had become the first man to stand on the world's highest mountain. His feat marked the end of an age of adventure. Explorers had plumbed the world's oceans, crossed its deserts, visited its poles. Now Everest, long a legend among the earth's unreachable places, had given up its mystery.

Perhaps that is why interest in the Everest expedition was worldwide. Nowhere was it stronger than in Great Britain. News of Hillary's achievement reached Britons just as they were celebrating the crowning of a new queen, Elizabeth II. British teams had been the first to try to climb Everest, and they had been trying for thirty-two years. Now, finally, a British team had succeeded. Hillary became a national hero. The fact that he came from New Zealand, halfway around the world, seemed not to matter at all.

One of the triumphal archways erected to honor the British Everest Expedition on their return from the climb. Crowds lined the route to welcome the mountaineers. The arch was decorated with flags of nations with which Nepal had diplomatic relations, and its apex represented Everest's peaks.

Hillary had expected that he would be getting some attention for his achievement before he got back to his bee business and more climbing. But the amount of attention he drew took him by surprise. On the long trek back to Kathmandu, runners brought letters of congratulations. Reporters and crowds of admirers met him on the trail. One newspaper reporter offered Hillary thousands of dollars for his story. (Hillary refused the offer. The expedition had sold exclusive story rights to the London *Times*.)

The most stunning news came in a letter from John Hunt, who had gone ahead to make travel arrangements. The queen of England had decided to honor him with a title. Ed Hillary, New Zealand beekeeper, was to become Sir Edmund Hillary, a British knight.

Tenzing did not lack for honors, either. They came from around the world. In Nepal and India, he was a celebrity. India made him its Director of Field Training at the Himalayan Mountaineering Institute in Darjeeling.

The expedition ended in grand style for Hillary and Tenzing. Important officials in Nepal and India held banquets in their honor. Crowds greeted them at airports. In London, the new queen knighted Hillary in the royal palace. Everyone wanted to meet him. Lecture tours took him to New Zealand and Australia, then across Europe, Britain, and the United States.

Tenzing waving a British flag from a mountaineer's ice pick after he, Hillary, and team leader John Hunt (left) arrived in London on July 3, 1953

Beneath a "canopy" of ice axes, Edmund and Louise Hillary leave Diocesan School Chapel in Auckland, New Zealand after their wedding.

Nevertheless, Hillary managed to take time out from the swirl of events for some very personal business. On his way back to New Zealand in August, he stopped in Australia to see a young woman named Louise Mary Rose. He knew her well. Although she was studying music in Sydney, Australia, she shared his interest in outdoor adventure. They were, in fact, in love. They returned to New Zealand for a September wedding—just in time for her to rush off with him on the lecture tour.

In later years, the entire Hillary family would take part in Ed's expeditions. But Louise stayed home early in 1954 when Hillary set off on his next Himalayan expedition. The goal this time was to explore the Barun Valley, a little-known region east of Everest. It was a jagged country of peaks and valleys, glaciers and gorges, dotted with massive unnamed peaks.

Hillary had visited the fringes of this territory with Eric Shipton in 1951. In 1952, after failing to conquer Cho Oyu, Hillary, Charles Evans, George Lowe, and Shipton had ventured into the Barun Valley. They had climbed a few of the Barun's countless peaks and gazed down upon huge valleys carpeted with wildflowers or choked with glaciers. Everest had been a higher priority for the next two years, but by 1954 Hillary was ready to return to the Barun.

New Zealand's Alpine Club sponsored the expedition. The plan was to map and photograph the region as well as climb some peaks. The expedition formed at Jogbani, a town that sits on Nepal's southern border with India. Trucks hauled the climbers and four tons of supplies to Dharan, where they hired fifteen Sherpa guides. They set off on foot on April 1, hiring porters along the way.

They spent most of April getting their expedition over a snowy pass to the Barun Valley. Finally they set up a base camp at 15,500 feet (4,724 meters). From there they planned to climb Makalu, towering more than two miles (3.2 kilometers) above them. The climbers began exploring their surroundings, looking for possible paths up Makalu. They split into separate groups and climbed some other peaks, getting used to the thin air and scouting the countryside.

Trouble came when Hillary, Jim McFarlane, and Brian Wilkins were climbing the second peak. While Hillary and five Sherpas were tending to camp chores, McFarlane and Wilkins climbed toward a pass for a view of Tibet. But they fell deep into a hidden crevasse. McFarlane was injured and could barely move. Wilkins was able to climb out and go back to camp for help.

The Himalayan peaks of Manaslu (26,648 feet; 8,122 meters) and Himalchuli (25,801 feet; 7,864 meters)

Crevasses in a Himalayan glacier

Hillary hurried to the crevasse with the Sherpas and some supplies. Sixty feet (18 meters) down in the hole was McFarlane. Tying on a rope, Hillary told the Sherpas to lower him into the icy chamber. But the cavity inside widened, and Hillary could not reach the walls to climb down and help McFarlane. Instead he dangled in the air, the rope around his chest squeezing his breath away.

The Sherpas tried to haul him out, but he became jammed under the overhanging lip of the crevasse. Hillary felt terrible pain in his sides as the Sherpas tugged to pull him free. Although he did not know it then, the rope had cracked three of his ribs. He struggled to the edge of the hole, and the Sherpas pulled him out.

Next they tried to lift McFarlane out. He, too, got jammed under the overhang. When it became too dark to continue, Hillary lowered two sleeping bags. Shortly McFarlane shouted up to the others, saying he had gotten inside the bags. Wearily, Hillary led the Sherpas back to camp.

They returned to the crevasse early the next morning. By now, Wilkins felt well enough to join the rescue team. On this attempt, it was Wilkins who descended into the crevasse.

Brian Wilkins (right), surrounded by curious onlookers, photographs the photographer after the expedition's descent from the Barun Valley in June 1954. At left, next to Hillary, is Dr. Michael Ball, the doctor on the expedition.

McFarlane was still alive, but he had not slept inside the sleeping bags after all—they only covered his knees. He was nearly frozen, and he seemed to have head and back injuries. Wilkins tied a sling around McFarlane, went back to the surface, and lowered a rope. McFarlane clipped it to the sling. They hauled him up, but he too became jammed under the overhang, even though the rescuers had chipped away ice to enlarge the opening. Finally, Hillary leaned far over the edge and pulled him free.

Hillary helps McFarlane onto a bed during a rest period on their downward trek.

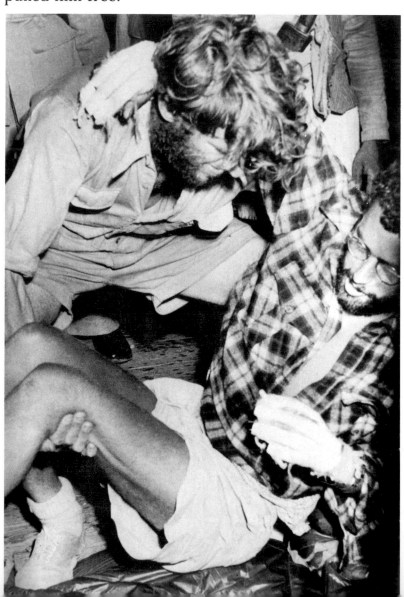

His hands bandaged and his legs inside a protective bag, McFarlane rides on a Sherpa's back.

McFarlane's clothes were frozen. "His hands . . . were whitish-blue and frozen stiff like claws. When we removed his boots his feet were hard and lifeless," Hillary wrote in *East of Everest,* his book about the expedition.

The rescuers lashed three pack frames together for a stretcher and lashed McFarlane to it on an air mattress. They needed to get him some medical attention as quickly as possible. His frozen hands and feet could become infected with gangrene, a deadly disease.

It took four days to get McFarlane back to base camp. Although he had many injuries and frostbite, Dr. Michael Ball, the expedition doctor, found his condition surprisingly good for all he had been through.

Shielding themselves from the rain, the descending party nears the town of Mulghat.

While Ball treated McFarlane in base camp, the others continued to explore the region. They decided to try to reach a col, over 23,000 feet (7,010 meters) high, that stretched between Makalu and another peak. Unaware of his broken ribs, Hillary ignored the pain in his chest. He reached camp with George Lowe, Norman Hardie, and Wilkins on May 16, but the next morning he felt too weak to stir from his tent. Hardie was also suffering from a bad headache. The two still did not feel well the next day. Hillary and Hardie decided to retreat to a lower camp while the others continued their climb.

But by now Hillary felt too weak to put on his boots. Lowe and Wilkins abandoned their planned climb, and everyone turned their attention to Hillary. They helped him pack up his gear. He started to walk, then suddenly passed out.

As Hillary later remembered, he sank into an awful spell of confused thinking and nightmares. Then he awoke to find himself on a stretcher, being carried down the mountain much as McFarlane had been. He felt better at the lower camps. His broken ribs had kept him from breathing properly, and at the higher elevations he had become oxygen starved.

Still, he was in better shape than McFarlane, whom they carried all the way back to Jogbani. The trek took twenty days. It took another week to get McFarlane back to Calcutta, where he could be flown to a hospital in New Zealand. He spent almost a year in the hospital, undergoing fifteen operations, including skin grafts and plastic surgery. By the time it was over, he had lost two fingers and parts of each foot.

The Himalayas had taken their toll.

The Himalayas: for many, the ultimate challenge; for some, the ultimate peril

63

Chapter 7
The Antarctic Trek

Even before Hillary's 1954 Himalayan expedition, the idea for an entirely different kind of adventure was growing in his mind. Late in 1953, George Lowe introduced Hillary to another famous explorer, Dr. Vivian Fuchs. Fuchs wanted to cross Antarctica, the icy continent covering the South Pole, by land.

The South Pole, like Mount Everest, had once been a great challenge for explorers. In 1911 Robert Scott, an Englishman, and Roald Amundsen, a Norwegian, set out for the pole in separate expeditions. Both were racing to be the first to reach the pole. Amundsen arrived first, and Scott got there five weeks later—but froze to death on his return trip. From 1914 to 1916, Sir Ernest Henry Shackleton had tried to travel all the way across Antarctica by land, but he had failed. Fuchs wanted to be the first to succeed.

Hillary met with Fuchs in Fuchs's London office. "I was immediately impressed by his forceful personality and his air of determination and confidence," Hillary wrote in *No Latitude for Error,* his account of the expedition. Fuchs quickly explained his plan.

Above: Ross Sea on Antarctica's Pacific Ocean side
Below: Hillary on a peak above New Zealand's Tasman Glacier, training for the Antarctic expedition

Two groups would work from opposite sides of the continent. On the Atlantic side, Fuchs's group would set up a base camp at the edge of the Weddell Sea on the Filchner Ice Shelf. On the Pacific side—the side closest to New Zealand—Hillary's group would set up a base at the edge of the Ross Sea. They would then send a team farther south to set up two large supply dumps. This would save Fuchs's team from having to carry all of its supplies on its long journey.

Antarctica is the world's fifth-largest continent, larger than the continental United States. In many ways, the challenges of crossing it were like those of an Everest expedition. Explorers would face severe cold, high winds, and long treks through barren wilderness. The New Zealand government and a private organization, the New Zealand Antarctic Society, together formed the

Ross Sea Committee to coordinate the expedition. The committee asked Hillary to lead.

His expedition sailed for Antarctica on December 15, 1956, with 500 tons (453,600 kilograms) of equipment. By the first of February the men had set up Scott Base, the expedition's headquarters. They set up their own supply dumps that they would use the next summer, then settled in for the long night of an Antarctic winter.

On October 14, 1957, Hillary and three others set out in four vehicles. Three were farm tractors, each with cleated, bulldozer-like treads and a small cabin for the driver. Each towed a sledge, or large sled, loaded with supplies. The fourth vehicle was a specially designed snow traveler called a Weasel. The Weasel towed the "caboose," a boxy, heated shelter. Several teams on dogsleds went ahead to scout their route.

Hillary (left) and companions Derek Wright and Murray Ellis wave from their tractors.

"Young" sea ice forming in pancake-like chunks off Antarctica

The explorers fought gale-force winds, bitter cold, and an endless series of crevasses as they climbed Antarctica's Skelton Glacier. Finally they reached the Polar Plateau, a massive ice cap that buries the Antarctic landmass under thousands of feet of ice. Once on top, they headed south to set up Fuchs's supply dumps.

Overcast skies and swirling snow made it hard for them to find their way. When the sun disappeared, snow and sky blended together in a featureless world of white. Magnetic compasses were not much help, because they lose their accuracy this close to the pole.

The true South Pole, or south geographic pole, is the point where the earth's lines of longitude meet. Magnetic compasses, however, are drawn to a different spot, over 1,500 miles (2,414 kilometers) away. Called the south magnetic pole, this point may shift as much as 5 miles (8 kilometers) in a year.

Whenever the sun appeared, the explorers checked its position. Then they used complicated mathematical tables to figure out their location. They also used the information to set an astrocompass, which then showed them their direction.

Even then, they wandered off course. At one point Hillary, suffering a fever, miscalculated their location. Another time, the astrocompass came loose from its mount, throwing off its accuracy. They discovered their mistakes and got back on course, but they had lost precious time and fuel.

They marked the site for the first supply dump on November 25. An airplane from Scott Base flew in some supplies to help them stock it. By December 6, they were ready to push farther south toward the pole.

On they struggled through soft snow and crevasse fields. The Weasel broke down for good on December

12. They stripped it of everything they could use and kept going. Ten miles (16 kilometers) from the site for the second supply dump, Hillary felt the back of his tractor sinking into a crevasse. Its nose tilted skyward, and he nearly fell out. He gunned the engine, the treads bit into the lip of the crevasse, and the machine heaved itself onto solid ground.

The group reached the second supply site on December 15. By now, they were 730 miles (1,175 kilometers) from Scott Base. This was past the halfway point of their journey. They were closer to the South Pole than to Scott Base.

Expedition co-leaders Hillary (left) and Dr. Vivian Fuchs (center), with U.S. Rear Admiral George Dufek, meet near the South Pole.

Hillary at the United States base on Ross Island, where New Zealand's flag is flown in his honor.

From the start of the expedition, Hillary had believed he and his team could be the first from New Zealand to reach the South Pole. Americans had set up a base there a year earlier, and large cargo planes kept it supplied. Once the New Zealand expedition reached the American base, Hillary reasoned, it could give its equipment to the Americans and fly out.

Members of the Ross Sea Committee had objected to this idea. They were worried that Hillary's exploration plans would get in the way of his most important duty, stocking Fuchs's supply dumps. But the headstrong Hillary had lugged extra supplies along. As soon as his team had Fuchs's second supply site stocked—five days after reaching the site—it set out for the pole.

First crevasses, then soft snow and altitude, slowed their progress. The Polar Plateau's surface rose gradually until they were above 10,000 feet (3,048 meters), and the thinning air made the tractor engines lose power. They cast off all but the bare necessities. Still, the fuel went at an alarming rate. Hillary knew his navigation would have to be perfect.

The American base appeared on the morning of January 4, 1958, only a little to the east of the course Hillary had set. The team stopped their tractors at a circle of drums and flagpoles that marked the South Pole. They ended their 1,250-mile (2,017-kilometer) journey with only enough fuel to go another 10 miles (16 kilometers).

Mists shrouding Antarctica's icy peaks

Hillary's team had been traveling for almost three months. The next day, in a U.S. Navy airplane, they recrossed that same distance in a few hours.

Fuchs still had not reached the South Pole. Bad surface conditions and time-consuming science experiments had put him behind schedule. Hillary did not think Fuchs would finish the journey across Antarctica before winter set in. He radioed the suggestion that Fuchs's team stop at the pole, leave its equipment, and resume the expedition the next summer.

But Fuchs's team pressed grimly on. It reached the pole on January 19 and rested only five days before continuing. Hillary flew to one of the supply dumps and joined the team, not as a leader but as an assistant and guide. The Fuchs expedition finished the crossing on March 22. Despite early setbacks, Fuchs's team had covered 2,158 miles (3,473 kilometers) in ninety-nine days.

Hillary returned to Antarctica nine years later, in October 1967. This expedition made the first ascent of Mount Herschell, an 11,000-foot (3,353-meter) peak on the northwest shore of the Ross Sea. Two teams chopped their way up vertical ice walls and steep slopes to reach the summit. As for Hillary, he worked with support teams, leaving the summit to younger climbers.

Antarctica held Hillary's interest, and he would visit there again in later years. But his life's work was in the Himalayas, and there he would spend some of his happiest—and most tragic—times.

Hillary at the end of his successful overland race to the South Pole

Chapter 8
Yetis, Experiments, and Schools

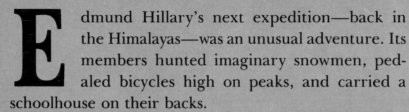

Edmund Hillary's next expedition—back in the Himalayas—was an unusual adventure. Its members hunted imaginary snowmen, pedaled bicycles high on peaks, and carried a schoolhouse on their backs.

In 1959, Field Enterprises Educational Corporation in Chicago, publisher of *World Book Encyclopedia,* filmed an educational television program about Hillary. During the project, Hillary told a Field executive about his latest idea for an expedition. He was interested in spending a winter high in the mountains while medical scientists studied how climbers' bodies adjusted to the thin air. After the winter, the expedition would try to climb Makalu, 27,790 feet (8,470 meters) high, without breathing gear. A French team had climbed it in 1955 using oxygen.

Picture from High in the Thin Cold Air.
© 1962 Field Enterprises Educational Corporation. Use by permission of World Book, Inc.

The climbers would also search for the fabled Abominable Snowman, a fearsome, ape-like animal said to live in the Himalayas. Sherpas had long believed in the creature. They called it *yeti.* Tales of yetis, told by various mountaineers, had captured the Western world's imagination. An expedition to search for a yeti was bound to draw worldwide interest, and Field Enterprises agreed to sponsor it.

September 1960 found Hillary in the Himalayas again. Other members of his expedition included experienced explorers from England, New Zealand, and the United States. To carry supplies, they hired more than 500 porters.

The expedition split into two groups. One went to find a site for a winter camp near Everest. Hillary led the other party west into the mysterious Rolwaling Valley in search of yetis. They brought with them binoculars, cameras, tape recorders, and even air rifles that fired drug-loaded darts so they could capture one.

The local people told them many yeti stories. A man from the village of Beding claimed that there was a yeti fur in the village. However, it turned out to be that of a Tibetan blue bear.

With Hillary was Desmond Doig, a journalist who knew the Sherpa people well. Together Doig and Hillary later wrote *High in the Thin Cold Air,* a book about this expedition. On October 15, Doig and a group of others found a set of yeti-like footprints on a glacier. Soon they found another. They followed them through sunlight and shadow. The tracks resembled small, four-footed animal tracks in the shade, but where warm sunlight melted the snow, the prints became enlarged and monster-like.

Returning east, Hillary, Doig, and the others reached

Footprints of a crow in the snow, photographed next to an ice axe to show their size. Small at first, the prints become greatly enlarged over time through the action of winds and melting snow.

From High in the Thin Cold Air.
© 1962 Field Enterprises Educational Corporation. Use by permission of World Book, Inc.

Khumjung on October 30. There they visited a monastery where Sherpas said a 200-year-old yeti scalp was kept. Expedition members examined the scalp and thought it had come from a serow, a Tibetan goat.

But the scalp still interested them. They arranged to borrow it for six weeks of scientific analysis in western nations. Hillary and Khunjo Chumbi, a Sherpa village elder, were in charge of the scalp. They walked 170 miles (274 kilometers) back to Kathmandu in nine days. Then they flew the scalp to scientists around the world—to Hawaii, the United States mainland, England, France, and back again.

Experts declared that the scalp was a fake, but indeed very old.

Scene from a December 1960 news conference at the Lincoln Park Zoo in Chicago, Illinois. Back from his Himalayan search for the yeti, Hillary watches his Nepalese guide, Khunjo Chumbi, display the scalp that was thought to be from a yeti.

No one in Hillary's group ever caught, saw, or heard a yeti. Hillary concluded that it does not exist, and no one has proved him wrong. Still, many people the world over continue to believe that there really is a gigantic Himalayan creature that local people call the yeti.

The scientific part of the expedition set up camp in Mingbo Valley, an area Hillary and Shipton had crossed in 1951. The leader was Norman Hardie, a New Zealand engineer and climber who had scaled 28,208-foot (8,598-meter) Mt. Kanchenjunga. More than 300 porters carried the material to build two large huts. The lower hut, called the Green Hut because of its green canvas cover, was set up on stone foundations at 17,500 feet (5,334 meters). The canvas was stretched over an insulated wooden frame.

Map of the Everest region
From High in the Thin Cold Air.
© *1962 Field Enterprises Educational Corporation. Use by permission of World Book, Inc.*

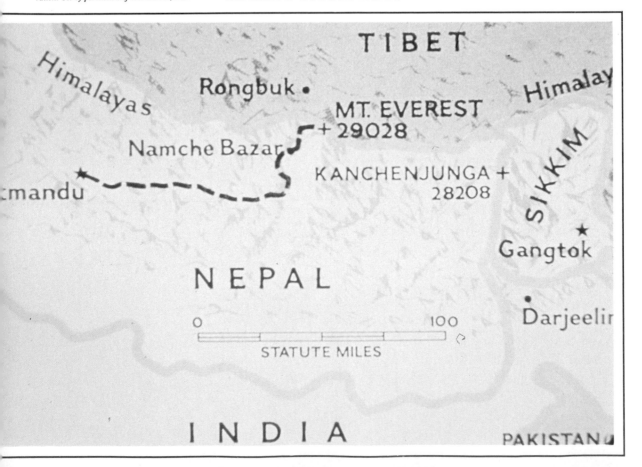

One of the participants in the bicycling experiment

From High in the Thin Cold Air.
© 1962 Field Enterprises Educational Corporation. Use by permission of World Book, Inc.

Higher up, they set up the Silver Hut. It was a 22-foot-long, 10-foot-wide (6.7-meter-long, 3-meter-wide) tube with a flat bottom for a floor. It was made of curved plywood panels with plastic foam insulation and an outer coat of silver paint.

The Silver Hut was more than a place to live. It was the laboratory for the experiments, too. A wind generator and storage batteries provided electricity for lights and equipment. A stationary exercise bicycle was used for the study. Subjects pedaled the bicycle while they breathed into an air tube. Scientists studied the chemicals in their breath. They also measured heart rate and blood pressure and analyzed blood samples. Each test told them something new about how the body works at high altitude.

Mingbo Valley's airstrip
From High in the Thin Cold Air.
© *1962 Field Enterprises Educational Corporation. Use by permission of World Book, Inc.*

Expedition members began to notice that more people were crowding into nearby villages. Many were refugees from Tibet who were fleeing the communist Chinese government, which had taken over their homeland. The International Red Cross was trying to get food and supplies into the area to help the refugees.

Hillary offered to level off a rough field for an airstrip in Mingbo Valley. In exchange, he suggested, his expedition would be allowed to make use of the plane. The Red Cross agreed. Soon it was able to fly in supplies, and Hillary had a way to move people between the remote valley and Kathmandu in a few hours.

After a winter of scientific studies, the assault on Makalu began in April. The climbers crossed a high ridge and set up a base camp at 17,600 feet (5,364 meters). They crossed two more high passes, a glacier, and a steep slope to a ridge on the north side of Makalu, the

Camp Four on Makalu
From High in the Thin Cold Air.
© *1962 Field Enterprises Educational Corporation. Use by permission of World Book, Inc.*

side away from Mingbo Valley. Then they began making advance camps up the side of the mountain.

On May 4, Hillary was suffering from a pounding headache and stayed in Camp Three. Two days later he moved down to Camp Two, but the next day he was worse. "I felt helpless, divorced from my limbs and, although perfectly rational, when I tried to say something it just came out as gibberish," he wrote in *High in the Thin Cold Air.*

On May 10, he retreated down the mountain with a Sherpa who was also ailing, until they were well below 15,000 feet (4,572 meters).

High on Makalu, the expedition was falling apart. Six Sherpas, tied together on a rope, fell down a slope. They all survived, but three were injured. At the same time, the climbers who had spent the winter in the Silver Hut were becoming ill.

Above: Dr. Tom Nevinson records data on John Harrison's physical condition during the Makalu climb. Below: The Makalu descent. Michael Gill (left), with frostbitten nose, follows a Sherpa who is carrying Peter Mulgrew.

These climbers were supposed to be fit after adjusting to the thin air. It turned out, however, that the strongest climbers on the expedition were two who had *not* spent the winter at high altitude—John Harrison, a New Zealand advertising agent, and Leigh Ortenburger, an American mathematician.

With the help of some Sherpa climbers, they organized a major evacuation and got everybody off the mountain. One climber, New Zealander Peter Mulgrew, had feet so severely frostbitten that surgeons had to amputate them.

The climbers had come within 400 feet (122 meters) of Makalu's summit without using oxygen, and some had done exercise bicycle tests as high as 25,800 feet (7,864 meters). But the Makalu expedition could not re-

ally be called a success. Hillary concluded that spending the winter at high altitude had not prepared the climbers for the Makalu assault. It had done just the opposite. On the one hand, they seemed to adjust well to life at 19,000 feet (5,791 meters). But they had also lost resistance to disease and were unable to get the heavy daily exercise they needed to stay in top shape. The Sherpas, in contrast, had adjusted to the thin air over many generations.

After the expedition, Hillary wrote, medical tests showed no lingering effects from his illness. From then on, however, he suffered every time he climbed at high altitudes.

Despite the Makalu disaster, the expedition was not over. It had a schoolhouse to build.

Hillary on the Makalu expedition, shortly before his descent

From High in the Thin Cold Air. © 1962 Field Enterprises Educational Corporation. Use by permission of World Book, Inc.

A Sherpa reads Hillary a petition from sixty children of the area, requesting that he build a school in Khumjung.

From High in the Thin Cold Air.
© *1962 Field Enterprises Educational Corporation. Use by permission of World Book, Inc.*

In Khumjung, where the yeti hunters had found the scalp, village elders had told Hillary that they wished they could afford a school for the village. He had proposed to build one in return for borrowing the scalp. Field Enterprises, the expedition's sponsor, had agreed to cover some costs, and the Indian Aluminum Company had donated aluminum sections for a one-room building. The Red Cross plane flew the sections to the Mingbo Valley airstrip.

In June, Hillary, several expedition members, and a group of Sherpas carried the sections to Khumjung on their backs and put up the schoolhouse. By June 12, the first class of Sherpa children were going to school and learning to read and write.

As Hillary was to learn, this was for him the beginning of a career of building schools, hospitals, bridges, and airfields for the people who would become his closest friends.

The success of the Khumjung school soon prompted other Sherpa villages to ask for schools. Hillary had an affection for the tough but friendly Sherpas. He counted many of them as close friends. Mountaineering was still important to Hillary, but now schools, hospitals, bridges, and water lines took more of his time.

Hillary had another reason for wanting to help. He was worried that China's communist government, which had taken over Tibet, would try to expand into Nepal. Military force was not the only way it might advance. The refugees from Tibet told stories of bad treatment by the Chinese, but they also told about new farms and schools that China was providing. Hillary felt that the best way to halt communist influence in the Himalayas was to offer aid programs from free nations.

However, Hillary did not believe that the usual kinds of aid programs would help the Sherpas. For example, he opposed a program that would send Sherpas to the United States to train them to be teachers. Sherpas who left the mountains to learn new skills might decide not to return to the hard life in the villages. If aid programs took the best Sherpas out of the villages, it would just make life worse for the rest. He decided to organize simple aid projects that would require the villagers to help themselves.

Hillary had taken consulting positions with both Field Enterprises and Sears, Roebuck and Company. He directed Field's operations in Australia, and he tested camping gear for Sears. Both companies agreed to back Hillary's Himalayan Schoolhouse Expedition in 1963.

This expedition would include five construction projects for villages in the Solu-Khumbu region. There would be schools for Thami and Pangboche, water pipelines for Khumjung and Khunde, and a temporary medical clinic in Khumjung, where two doctors would stay and treat Sherpas' ailments for six months.

Besides the construction projects, the expedition would also climb the peaks Taweche, 21,463 feet (6,542 meters), and Kangtega, 22,340 feet (6,809 meters). The peaks overlook the villages and flank the Everest trail.

The expedition included some climbers from the Makalu group. Among these were Bhanu Bannerjee, an interpreter and photographer; Desmond Doig, the journalist; and Dr. Michael Gill, a physician. Murray Ellis, a New Zealander who had been with Hillary in the Antarctic, went along as construction engineer and mountaineer. Phillip Houghton was another New Zealander and a physician. Jim Wilson was an ordained Presbyterian minister from New Zealand. From the United States came Dave Dornan and Tom Frost, both mountain climbers who also knew construction work.

In March 1963, Hillary and the others hauled tons of equipment to Khumjung. Sherpas who had become their friends on the last expedition greeted them with a big feast. They were happy to find the Khumjung school busy and the students learning eagerly.

They were not happy to find that a medical crisis was brewing in Khumjung. A Sherpa had become ill with smallpox, a deadly disease, and it had spread from one village to another. Signs of an epidemic were just appearing when Hillary's expedition arrived.

To stem the epidemic, the Sherpas needed a vaccine that makes people immune to the disease. Hillary radioed for emergency supplies, and a Red Cross plane

Examining a Sherpa patient at the Khumjung clinic

From High in the Thin Cold Air.
© 1962 Field Enterprises Educational Corporation. Use by permission of World Book, Inc.

dropped a package of the vaccine two days later. Runners carried more from Kathmandu. The expedition doctors taught other expedition members and some Sherpas how to give vaccinations, and they all began traveling through the villages. At least twenty-five Sherpas died from smallpox, but Hillary's expedition vaccinated more than 7,000 people, saving them from a worse disaster.

Even without the smallpox crisis, the Khumjung clinic was busy. With no hospitals or clinics, the death rate was high among Sherpa children. Many disease problems were caused simply by a lack of knowledge about disease or about the need for cleanliness. Sherpas often blamed illnesses on supernatural forces or witchcraft.

Doctors at the Khumjung clinic treated routine cases of dog bites and broken bones, but they also saw Sherpas with cancer and heart disease. Unfortunately, the doctors could not save everyone.

The clinic's purpose was not just to treat Sherpas for a few months. It also included gathering information about the Sherpas' medical needs. The information would be used to plan a permanent hospital for the region.

One way to deal with illness is to prevent it. Clean drinking water helps prevent the spread of many diseases. Hillary and a crew built a small dam to collect water at a spring high above Khumjung and laid a plastic pipeline down the steep hillside. Villagers built a wall of rocks down the hillside to protect the pipe and used stone and concrete to build collecting tanks in the village. A similar water system was built for the village of Khunde.

Just as important as health care, Hillary believed, was education. With better health care, the Sherpa population would grow. A larger population would require more food, and that would require better farming methods. It would be hard to learn such things without some ability to read and write.

The 1963 expedition built its first school in Pangboche. They opened it with a big ceremony on April 29. The school began with fifty-four students. Included with the children were two grown men who were not about to miss this chance to learn.

The expedition built the second school in the village of Thami, the birthplace of Hillary's Everest partner, Tenzing Norgay. Thami is the only village between Namche Bazar and the Nangpa La, a 19,000-foot (5,791-meter) pass between Nepal and communist

Young students at the Pangboche school

Tibet. Many Tibetans had fled over the pass to Thami. The school built there in April and May 1963 reflected a blend of cultures. It had a Western-made aluminum roof, rock walls, and Sherpa and Tibetan decorations. The grand opening was held on May 27. The head lama (monk) from Thyangboche Monastery attended, bringing a great honor to the village.

The success of the Khumjung school had encouraged the Nepalese government to open schools in Namche Bazar, Chaunrikharka, and Junbesi. All the schools would be part of a government school system in the Himalayas. The government also arranged to take over the schools that Hillary's expeditions had built.

With these construction projects completed, Hillary's expedition members were eager to climb the Taweche and Kangtega peaks. Taweche towers over Pangboche and the Thyangboche Monastery. It did not look too hard to climb, but the climbers met with one nasty obstacle after another. The summit ridge was a frightening series of overhanging cornices and slabs of snow poised to avalanche 6,000 feet (1,829 meters). Less than 200 feet (61 meters) from the top, they decided not to attempt the summit. To honor the gods that local people believed dwelled in the mountain, they planted prayer flags from the Thyangboche Monastery and retreated.

Kangtega's great rock walls presented a terrible face to the Khumbu region. But it had a weak southern flank that Hillary had spotted during the winter expedition. Dornan, Frost, Gill, and Wilson led the assault on Kangtega with five Sherpas. The route led up an icefall to steep slopes covered with deep snow. Near the summit, a great chunk of snow slid away from between Gill and Wilson as they climbed. Luckily, it took no one with it. They reached the top after that.

The Lukla airstrip

The Schoolhouse Expedition ended on June 7. As Hillary's group left Khumjung, the children cheered and waved. Expedition members had built more than schools and pipelines in the Sherpa villages; they had built friendships as well.

Hillary was back in the region the following year with another expedition. This time they built a dirt airstrip at 9,000 feet (2,743 meters) near Lukla, a village along the Dudh Kosi River south of Namche Bazar. The airstrip made it possible to bring people and supplies to the edge of the Everest region quickly. Expedition members also built bigger and stronger bridges over the Dudh Kosi and Bhote Kosi rivers near Namche Bazar.

Hillary, later accompanied by his wife and children, would lead other construction expeditions to the Himalayas. By 1971, Hillary and others had helped build eleven schools and the area's first hospital.

Hillary poses with lamas and other villagers at the Risingo Monastery.
From High in the Thin Cold Air.
© *1962 Field Enterprises Educational Corporation. Use by permission of World Book, Inc.*

Chapter 9
A Family Adventure

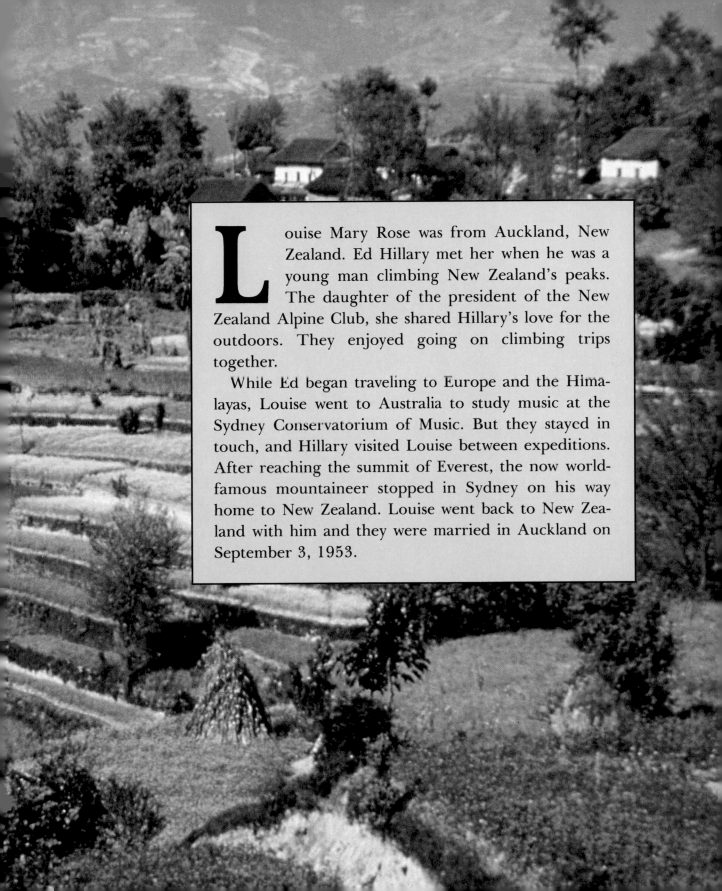

Louise Mary Rose was from Auckland, New Zealand. Ed Hillary met her when he was a young man climbing New Zealand's peaks. The daughter of the president of the New Zealand Alpine Club, she shared Hillary's love for the outdoors. They enjoyed going on climbing trips together.

While Ed began traveling to Europe and the Himalayas, Louise went to Australia to study music at the Sydney Conservatorium of Music. But they stayed in touch, and Hillary visited Louise between expeditions. After reaching the summit of Everest, the now world-famous mountaineer stopped in Sydney on his way home to New Zealand. Louise went back to New Zealand with him and they were married in Auckland on September 3, 1953.

Hillary with his wife, Louise, and their children (left to right) Peter, Belinda, and Sarah in 1962

The following spring Hillary returned to the Himalayas to explore the Barun Valley. When he returned to New Zealand, he and Louise built a house and had their first two children, Peter and Sarah. Their third child, Belinda, was born after Ed's 1956–1958 Antarctic expedition. That adventure had kept Hillary away from his family for more than a year, including two Christmas holidays. Afterwards he turned down invitations to lecture in England so he could spend time at home with his family.

Louise described herself in the first of several books she wrote, *Keep Calm If You Can*: "I'm just a common, garden-variety sort of wife. The cabbage kind, not the long-suffering pioneer type." It was a modest description, but hardly accurate. In the early years of her marriage, she spent months at a time alone while her husband traveled in the Himalayas. She raised their three children. When they were old enough to travel, she closed up the house and led her tribe halfway around the world, in and out of strange airports, and on foot through the wild Himalayas. She did this while nursing children's colds, keeping track of belongings, and dealing with reporters who wanted to know what it was like to be the wife of a famous explorer. She also found time to write books about her travels.

The first trip to the Himalayas for Louise and the children was at the end of November 1966. They flew from New Zealand to Kathmandu, then boarded a small aircraft for the 100-mile (161-kilometer) flight to the Lukla airstrip. From there they hiked up the Dudh Kosi valley to Khunde, where Hillary's expedition had just finished building the region's first hospital. The family of Dr. Max Pearl, the hospital project's medical director, went with them.

For the hospital's grand opening on December 18, important officials from Nepal, New Zealand, Great Britain, and the United States flew in by helicopter. A Buddhist lama blessed the building, walking around it and throwing sacred rice at the foundation.

On this trip and others, the Hillary family lived much like the Sherpas. According to Louise Hillary's book *A Yak for Christmas,* the children ate curds from yak milk and called it "Himalayan ice cream." With every trip, they grew closer to their Sherpa friends. The trips were not easy, and they had to pay their own expenses. For one expedition they sold their piano, no doubt a real sacrifice for music-loving Louise.

The Dalai Lama's quarters at Jokang Temple, Lhasa, Tibet

Above: Kathmandu, Nepal
Below: Women at Bodnath Temple, Kathmandu

From Khunde, Ed took his family on the long trek to the Everest base camp. He hadn't been there since 1953, and he wanted to show the place to his wife and children. The children packed their own warm clothes, sleeping bags, and ice axes for the trip. He led them up a peak to a height of 18,300 feet (5,578 meters) where they could look up the Khumbu Icefall into the Western Cwm, the valley of ice and rock that led to Everest.

Louise found no glorious sight in Everest. She thought of it as "an ugly, ungraceful lump" among other beautiful peaks. "Yet there is something rather terrifying about its dark brooding shape," she wrote.

At the end of 1971, Louise and the children joined Ed on a Sherpa aid project. Peter was now 17, Sarah was 15, and Belinda was 13. The family stayed with the ambassador to Nepal in Kathmandu until Hillary came down out of the mountains to meet them.

They all trekked together back to Junbesi, where work was just starting on a middle school. Louise and the children joined the villagers in hauling rocks for the school's walls. They carried the heavy stones with bamboo baskets and headbands. Eventually the Solu district, part of the Solu-Khumbu region south of Namche Bazar, asked for a hospital like the one at Khunde. With 20,000 people in this region, the need was real.

The hospital project gave Ed and Louise a reason to do something they had talked about for years. They would move the whole family to Nepal and live in Kathmandu for a year. In 1975, the year they moved, Ed was 55, Louise was 44, and the children were 21, 19, and 17. Each of them had interests to pursue. Ed went to the village of Phaphlu to start work on the hospital project. Sarah returned to New Zealand to take university courses. Peter and a friend left to travel in India. Belinda, the youngest, stayed with Louise in Kathmandu.

Child wood-carriers in the village of Namche Bazar, Nepal

Edmund and Louise Hillary with mountaineer George Lowe (right)

Louise and Belinda were to join Hillary at the end of March. The rebuilt airfield at Phaphlu would allow them to take an airplane directly to the village from Kathmandu. On March 31, 1975, as Hillary waited for them at the airfield, he sensed something was wrong. The aircraft he saw approaching was not an airplane, but a helicopter. The pilot brought bad news: The airplane carrying Louise and Belinda had crashed during takeoff. When Hillary reached the scene of the crash, he found that his wife and youngest child were dead.

Hillary had had a busy schedule. Now he continued it, working on the hospital and making appearances in Europe and the United States. The schedule gave him things to do; it kept him from dwelling on his loss.

The Himalayas

His Sherpa friends worried that he would not want to return. Hillary felt, however, that if he did not finish the hospital, it would mean that his wife and daughter had lost their lives for nothing. The hospital was finished in May 1976, and high officials came from several countries to celebrate its opening.

With the project finished, Hillary found himself wondering what to do with his life. After spending a quarter-century on Himalayan expeditions and aid projects, his future suddenly seemed unclear. But Hillary thought again about a project that he and Louise had discussed in years past. It was an expedition that at first sounds impossible.

Hillary decided to climb the Himalayas in a boat.

Chapter 10
The Last Ascent

In India flows a great river called the Ganges. It spreads itself across the wide, flat plains of northern India and Bangladesh, finally emptying into the Indian Ocean at the Bay of Bengal. Many rivers flow into the Ganges along the way. Among the rivers feeding it are those that drain the mighty glaciers of the Himalayas.

Ed and Louise had talked of traveling up the Ganges from the sea to the foot of the mountains, then continuing up the mountains to the river's ultimate source—the sky. After Louise's death, Hillary decided to turn the idea into reality with an expedition in 1977.

Hillary had had some experience on Himalayan rivers. In 1968, he had organized a small, two-week expedition to travel up 90 miles (145 kilometers) of wild water on the Sun Kosi River in Nepal.

They had used a new kind of boat called a jet boat. Instead of a propeller, the jet boat uses a high-powered pump to push a jet of water behind it. Because it has no propeller, it can go through very shallow water.

The Ganges expedition would cover 1,500 miles (2,414 kilometers) from the Bay of Bengal to the city of Deoprayag. There the foaming Bhagirathi and Alaknanda rivers plunge down from the mountains to form the Ganges. At the head of the Alaknanda River is the village of Badrinath, the site of a holy Hindu shrine. Hillary had visited Badrinath on his first Himalayan expedition in 1951. Now he would try to reach the village with three jet boats.

Most Indians follow the Hindu religion. Hindus believe the Ganges is a holy river that flows down from their gods. Hindus travel up the Ganges on journeys called pilgrimages to visit holy places. The jet-boat expedition would also travel up the Ganges and visit holy places—making a journey like a pilgrimage itself.

The expedition would be a measure of Hillary's reputation. It had been nearly twenty-five years since he had climbed Mount Everest, but he was still respected. The government of India and several of the nation's largest companies helped pay for the expedition. All along the route, government officials and local leaders wanted to meet him. Despite his isolation as a child, Hillary was able to develop friendships with all kinds of people, from poor Sherpa peasants to high government officials.

The official name of the expedition was the Indo-New Zealand Ganga Expedition. It had 19 members, including Hillary's son, Peter, and many old friends. Peter shared his father's zest for mountains. He would be one of the climbers scouting a route up 19,600-foot (5,974-meter) Narayan Parbat, the peak they planned to attempt after the boat trip.

The trip began in the Bay of Bengal, where the Ganges empties into the Indian Ocean across vast, flat deltas. Their route followed a wild maze of shallow

Indians bathing in the Ganges

channels that were home to ferocious Bengal tigers and poisonous snakes. The Indian government has turned part of the region into a tiger sanctuary to preserve the beautiful beasts from hunters.

From the safety of their boats, the travelers saw a tiger as it swam across a channel ahead of them. It reached shore and vanished among the trees. Moments later, another tiger strode into view. It glared at the men with no trace of fear in its eyes, then gave a soft, deep growl and walked away.

Rice paddies are seen throughout South and Southeast Asia. These people are planting rice in a paddy in Java, Indonesia.

The swamps gave way to the rice paddies of Indian farms as the expedition headed upstream. After a thousand miles (1,609 kilometers), the rice paddies along the shore gave way to pastures as the land grew higher. Soon the first rapids appeared. Each day the rapids grew bigger, wilder, and more dangerous. Hillary learned that finding safe routes through the rapids was as important and sometimes as difficult as finding safe routes up mountains. On some rapids, a boat would disappear entirely under white foaming water, only to reappear magically with no one lost overboard.

Hillary found the expedition attracting far more attention than he had expected. Indians lined the river by the thousands in larger cities. Even in rural areas, people came to the river banks to see the three boats.

Everywhere, people surprised Hillary with their friendliness. "While planning the expedition, I had been worried that our boats would be resented as noisy intruders on the holy river, yet everywhere we were welcomed as heroes and accepted as pilgrims undertaking a meritorious journey," he wrote in *From the Ocean to the Sky*, his account of the expedition.

They reached Deoprayag on September 25 and started up the Alaknanda River. They passed the city of Nandaprayag on September 29 and came to a waterfall, which they called the Nandaprayag Falls. The expedition had traveled 1,500 miles (2,414 kilometers) on water in six weeks. It was impossible for the boats to climb the waterfall, so Hillary decided it was time to continue on foot.

Peter Hillary and his climbing partner, Murray Jones, had left the boats earlier. They had gone ahead to Badrinath to scout routes up Narayan Parbat. They had found steep rock faces and knife-edged ridges with no easy way up. When Hillary's party arrived, Peter and Murray suggested a switch. Instead of fearsome Narayan Parbat, the expedition could climb nearby Nar Parbat, a much easier peak just over 19,000 feet (5,791 meters).

They hired local porters and set up a base camp at about 15,000 feet (4,572 meters). The next day, October 12, they all hauled loads up to a higher camp. Although Ed Hillary was still strong, it exhausted him to carry a pack up to the plateau at 18,000 feet (5,486 meters). He was pushing too hard without waiting for his body to get used to the altitude. He spent the next day in his tent.

The next morning he was ill, in pain, and could barely wake up. Mike Gill, a doctor who had been with Hillary on the schoolhouse and other expeditions, decided Hillary needed to get to a lower altitude fast.

Murray Jones hurried ahead to call for a helicopter while others carried Hillary down a steep, snow-filled gully. Hillary improved as they descended. The helicopter came the next morning and sped away with Hillary and Gill.

It flew them to a military hospital far from the mountains. Hillary and Gill spent two days there, but their minds were on the expedition. They finally persuaded hospital officials to order a helicopter to return them as far as Joshimath, a town near Badrinath but at a lower elevation.

The expedition was still going strong. A group of climbers that included Peter Hillary reached the summit of Nar Parbat on October 17. The next day, they climbed another peak, Akash Parbat.

After the summit climbs, they performed one last act to conclude the expedition. They set a small copper bottle on a stove. Inside the bottle was water they had taken from the Bay of Bengal, now frozen from the cold of the mountain. When it thawed, they poured it out on a mound of snow. The ocean had reached the sky.

Although Hillary was still sad over the deaths of his wife and youngest child, he did not let depression rule him. He continued to busy himself with Himalayan projects. The bridges, schools, and hospitals he had helped build over the years had to be maintained, repaired, or rebuilt.

He had a scare in October 1979. His son, Peter, then 24, was on an expedition to climb an avalanche-scoured face of Ama Dablam. While working at the hospital in

Phaphlu, Hillary got word that someone had died in an accident on the mountain. Hillary caught a plane to Syangboche, a small airstrip near Khunde, and hiked to the hospital there. A helicopter was bringing in the Ama Dablam expedition members. Peter was with them—suffering a broken arm, but alive.

Soon Ed Hillary was to face a crisis of his own on a familiar peak—Mount Everest.

In 1980, an American expedition received permission from the People's Republic of China to climb Mount Everest from Tibet. It would be the first American expedition to attempt the "impossible" east face of the great mountain. Hillary was asked to help manage the expedition. He agreed, ignoring the troubles he had had at high altitudes.

Tibetan village women on an Everest trek

Hillary was eager to see the east face of Everest again. It was a great wall of ice that towered over a beautiful valley. He had seen it in 1953, from atop the South Col. Now he hoped to see it from the valley itself.

The expedition flew to Tibet on August 15, 1981. Then it headed overland in trucks and a bus, grinding over high mountain passes for several days before reaching Kharta at 12,474 feet (3,802 meters). There the expedition gathered yaks and porters, loaded them with supplies, and set out on foot on August 23.

They reached base camp on August 28. It offered a spectacular view of Everest's east face and other great peaks. Hillary and his son Peter, in their book *Ascent,* called it "perhaps one of the most spectacular base camps in the world." A series of ice cliffs threatened avalanches all along the east face. The expedition hoped to find a fairly safe way right up the middle.

At base camp, Hillary began having headaches. On September 1, the expedition's physician, Dr. Jim Morrissey, advised Hillary to get to a lower altitude. The two walked down to a spot 2,000 feet (610 meters) below base camp. There Hillary set up a little camp for himself and kept company with the expedition's yaks and an occasional visitor. After a week, he felt better and returned to base camp.

His improvement did not last, however. On September 18, Hillary became ill again, but this time he was vomiting, seeing double, and feeling terrible pain in his chest. By the next morning, he did not know where he was and could not speak clearly. Morrissey quickly made packs for an emergency evacuation to a lower altitude.

It was a terrible trip. They passed the yak camp where Hillary had just spent a week, but Hillary did not recognize it. At one point he saw a large rock along a stream

Hillary, ill from this climb, being airlifted to safety

and thought it was a truck coming for them. Later, a yak ran wild and cut Hillary on the head with its horn.

From Kharta, Hillary traveled back the way he had come, crossing China and finally reaching New Zealand. His headaches gradually faded away.

On the mountain, deep snow brought the expedition to a halt. The loose snow created a threat of deadly avalanches. Still more than 7,000 feet (2,134 meters) from the summit, they had to retreat.

Some of the expedition's members got a second chance. They formed the core of another American expedition to the east face in 1983, and this time they reached the summit. But the 1981 expedition was Hillary's last in the high Himalayas.

Chapter 11
Preserving the Wilderness

In 1953, on Hillary's Everest expedition, the Himalayan wilderness had seemed limitless and unspoilable. Nobody worried about littering or cutting wood from the juniper forests that carpeted the high valleys. "On our 1953 Everest expedition we just threw our empty tins and any trash into a heap on the rubble-covered ice at Base Camp. We cut huge quantities of the beautiful juniper shrub for our fires," Hillary wrote in a book he edited, *Ecology 2000: The Changing Face of Earth.*

But nothing on earth is limitless. The mighty Himalayan wilderness is fragile. Its slow-growing forests have not been able to keep up with the fast-growing population of Sherpas who need wood for fuel and shelter. Mountaineers and trekkers have taken a share of the natural resources, too. People have thinned or stripped away wide areas of forest, leaving little shelter for wildlife and baring the thin soil. Heavy rains have washed away the soil, destroying farm fields and grazing pastures.

When Hillary first visited the Everest region in 1951, he marveled at the lush evergreen forests that filled the Dudh Kosi river valley from Chaunrikharka to Namche Bazar. Trekking past the Thyangboche Monastery to Pangboche and on to the foot of the Khumbu Glacier, he noted that pine trees gave way to short but hardy juniper and then to grassy pastures.

Things changed slowly at first, as Nepal opened its borders to outsiders. With their achievement on Everest, Hillary and Tenzing drew attention to the region. More people came to visit.

The expeditions themselves had a big impact. At first Hillary saw only the good things his projects brought. In 1963, for example, he learned that the 1961 winter expedition had helped save the people of Pangboche from a potato crop failure. The expedition had not brought food, but it had paid the Pangboche villagers to build the little airstrip for the Red Cross plane. The money had enabled them to buy food.

But Hillary's projects brought other changes, too, that were not as positive.

His 1964 expedition included a project to build an airstrip near the village of Lukla, south of Namche Bazar. The airstrip helped his aid projects by making it easier to bring supplies and people into the Everest region. But the little airstrip also opened the region to tourists unwilling to hike all the way from Kathmandu.

Tourists created a demand for hotels, restaurants, and stores. Development brought jobs and business for the Sherpas, but it also took away the beauty and solitude of the region. It also increased the demand on the region's sparse resources. Sherpas found they could make money selling firewood to trekkers. They began cutting down trees without replacing them.

Hillary and John Hunt (front left and right) meeting in England in 1978 for a reunion with other members of the 1953 Everest expedition

These were changes that Hillary did not like, and he realized he was partly to blame. "At times I am racked by a sense of guilt," he wrote in his autobiography, *Nothing Venture, Nothing Win.*

The changes spread from Lukla to Namche Bazar and on toward Everest. Trekking past Khunde in early 1972, the Hillary family saw workers turning a once-peaceful meadow into an airstrip. A hotel was also under construction. The tourist industry was coming to the once-remote villages of Khunde and Khumjung, where Hillary had started his schoolhouse and hospital projects.

The Thyangboche Monastery had once been a quiet, peaceful place for Buddhist monks, set among towering, ice-cloaked peaks. Now it was a tourist spot.

Worse, tourism was affecting the delicate natural balance in the high country of the Khumbu district. Louise described her concern in her last book, *High Time:* "In the upper Khumbu the dark green, prostrate juniper and the azalea bushes have been hacked away slowly by advancing armies of tourists and climbers as they puff their way towards the foot of Everest. There is probably time for the Everest region to be saved by making it a national park, patrolled by highly trained rangers. But this must happen soon." A national park was established, but not before Louise Hillary's death in 1975.

In 1973, Ed Hillary began working with the United Nations and Nepal's national parks office to try to reverse, or at least stop, the destruction. But Nepal was a small nation with little money to create and manage a park in the Himalayas. Hillary knew his own country had a good national park system to protect its mountains. He went to New Zealand's ministry of foreign affairs and asked for help.

The response was quick. The New Zealand government sent a three-man team to Nepal to study the problem. It assigned a national park adviser to Nepal in 1975, agreed to provide funds for five years, helped Nepal create a management plan, and trained the first Nepalese park warden.

Nepal officially opened Sagarmatha National Park in 1976, putting 480 square miles (1,243 square kilometers) under government protection. Sagarmatha is the Nepalese name for Mount Everest. Mount Everest is the park's centerpiece. The visitor's center for the park is at Namche Bazar, now more than ever the gateway to Everest.

Creating a national park did not suddenly solve the region's problems. In 1981, Hillary repeated his first

Hillary in West Berlin in 1988 after receiving the Golden Camera, a West German television award

trip to the site of Everest Base Camp and found the once-forested land beyond Pangboche almost bare. The problems will take a long time to heal, and much effort will be needed just to stop the damage from getting worse.

Hillary's fame as the first person on Everest and his many aid projects have won him respect and friendship around the world. He has used his influence to try to help the mountains and their people, the Sherpas. Although he never sought honors, the former beekeeper has earned them over the years. His knighthood came in 1953 for climbing the world's highest mountain. In 1985, New Zealand added another: It named him its ambassador to India and Nepal.

Appendices

Opposite page: Members of the British Mount Everest Expedition snaking their way up the snowy mountainside

Photo from High in the Thin Cold Air. © *1962 Field Enterprises Educational Corporation. Use by permission of World Book, Inc.*

Above: Hillary with a Sherpa villager. To support his Sherpa aid projects and, later, the restoration of natural resources in the Everest region, Hillary established the Himalayan Trust, a nonprofit organization based in New Zealand. For information about the trust, write to:

Himalayan Trust Board
278A Remuera Road
Auckland, New Zealand

Kathmandu, Nepal, June 1953: Edmund Hillary settles down to read some long-awaited mail from home after his descent from Mount Everest.

Tenzing Norgay and Edmund Hillary pose proudly
after being honored by Nepal's King Tribhuvana.
Tenzing was presented with the Nepal Tara (Nepal
Star), First Class, and Hillary received the honor of
Gurkja Dakshina Bahu (Mighty Right Arm of the
Gurkhas), First Class.

Timeline of Events in Hillary's Lifetime

1919—Edmund Percival Hillary is born in Auckland, New Zealand

1921—George Mallory leads a British Everest expedition, losing his life in the attempt

1936—Hillary goes into his father's beekeeping business

1944—During World War II, Hillary joins the New Zealand Air Force and serves as a navigator in the South Pacific

1947—With mountaineer Harry Ayres, Hillary climbs New Zealand's Mount Cook

1951—Hillary participates in Eric Shipton's expedition to scout a route up Mount Everest

1952—Hillary joins a British expedition to climb Cho Oyu, a peak west of Everest, in training for an Everest climb; a Swiss expedition attempts Mount Everest

1953—Edmund Hillary and Sherpa Tenzing Norgay reach the summit of Mount Everest on an expedition sponsored by the Royal Geographical Society and the Alpine Club; Queen Elizabeth II of Great Britain knights Hillary for his achievement; Hillary marries Louise Mary Rose in Auckland, New Zealand

1954—Hillary leads an unsuccessful expedition to climb Mount Makalu in the Barun Valley

1955—Hillary publishes *High Adventure*, an account of the Everest climb

1958—As part of Sir Vivian Fuchs's transantarctic expedition, Hillary completes a trek from Antarctica's Ross Sea coast to the South Pole

1960—Hillary begins an expedition to climb Mount Makalu; the expedition includes testing the climbers' high-altitude physical condition and searching for the yeti, or Abominable Snowman

1961—Hillary publishes *No Latitude for Error*, an account of the Antarctic expedition

1962—Hillary publishes *High in the Thin Cold Air* about the Makalu expedition

1963—On the Himalayan Schoolhouse Expedition, Hillary and others embark on construction projects to build schools, clinics, and other facilities in Himalayan villages

1967—Hillary takes part in an Antarctic expedition to climb Mount Herschell

1975—A plane crash claims the lives of Hillary's wife, Louise, and daughter Belinda; Hillary's autobiography, *Nothing Venture, Nothing Win*, is published

1976—The Nepalese government opens Sagarmatha National Park, which encompasses Mount Everest

1977—Hillary leads an expedition up the Ganges River from the Bay of Bengal to its source in the Himalayas

1979—Hillary publishes *From the Ocean to the Sky*, describing the Ganges expedition

1981—Climbing on the Tibet side, Hillary participates in an attempt on Mount Everest's east face

1985—New Zealand appoints Hillary as its ambassador to India and Nepal

Glossary of Terms

avalanche—A falling mass of snow, ice, or rock down a mountainside or other steep slope

belay—To secure a rope to a mountain with a cleat or pin to prevent a climber from falling

Buddhist—A person who follows the beliefs and practices of Buddhism, a religion based on the teachings of Gautama Buddha

col—A saddle-shaped dip in the ridge between two mountain peaks

cornice—An overhanging, wave-like formation of snow shaped by wind; dangerous because no earth lies beneath the seemingly solid snow

couloir—A gorge in the side of a mountain

crampon—A device with sharp points that mountaineers wear over their boots for climbing on steep snow and ice

crevasse—A deep, narrow opening or crack in a glacier; crevasses open and close with the movement of the underlying river of ice

cwm—(pronounced "coom") A bowl-shaped valley enclosed or flanked by mountains

frostbite—Injury due to freezing of surface tissues, most commonly occurring on the nose, ears, fingers, or toes; can be severe enough to call for amputation of the frozen body part

glacier—A large body of ice that moves slowly down a valley or spreads across land; it is actually a frozen river

Hindu—A person who follows the beliefs and practices of Hinduism, a religion practiced in India and neighboring countries that emphasizes religious duties, rituals, and meditation

icefall—A mass of broken and unstable ice where a glacier makes a steep drop; it is a frozen waterfall

monastery—A house for monks or other people who belong to a religious order and have taken religious vows

monsoon—A season of storms, or a storm in the monsoon season, on the Indian subcontinent and in the Himalayas. In India the monsoon comes as rain; in the Himalayas it comes as snow.

pilgrimage—A journey to a shrine or other holy place

serac—A block of ice in a glacier

Sherpa—A people, originally from Tibet, who live in the high Himalayas

sledge—A sled-like vehicle with low runners used to transport loads over ice

vaccine—A treatment that increases a person's resistance to a disease

yak—A Tibetan ox

yeti—Sherpa name for an ape-like creature thought by some to live in the Himalayan Mountains, but whose existence is not supported by scientific evidence

Bibliography

For further reading, see:

Hillary, Edmund. *East of Everest*. NY: E. P. Dutton, 1956.

Hillary, Edmund. *From the Ocean to the Sky*. NY: Viking Press, 1979.

Hillary, Edmund. *High Adventure*. NY: E. P. Dutton, 1955.

Hillary, Edmund. *No Latitude for Error*. NY: E. P. Dutton, 1961.

Hillary, Edmund. *Nothing Venture, Nothing Win*. NY: Coward, McCann & Geoghegan, 1975.

Hillary, Edmund. *Schoolhouse in the Clouds*. Garden City, NY: Doubleday, 1964.

Hillary, Edmund, editor. *Ecology 2000: The Changing Face of Earth*. NY: Beaufort Books, 1984.

Hillary, Edmund, and Doig, Desmond. *High in the Thin Cold Air*. Garden City, NY: Doubleday, 1962.

Hillary, Edmund, and Hillary, Peter. *Ascent*. Garden City, NY: Doubleday, 1986.

Hillary, Louise, *A Yak for Christmas*. Garden City, NY: Doubleday, 1969.

Hillary, Louise. *High Time*. Garden City, NY: Doubleday, 1973.

Kohli, M. S. *Nine Atop Everest: Story of the Indian Ascent*. Port Washington, NY: Kennikat, 1969.

May, Julian. *Hillary and Tenzing: Conquerors of Mt. Everest*. Sacramento, CA: Creative Editions, 1972. For grades 2-5.

Unsworth, Walt. *Everest: A Mountaineering History*. Boston: Houghton Mifflin, 1981.

Index

Picture Identifications for Chapter Opening Spreads

6-7—Mount Everest

10-11—Mount Cook (center) in New Zealand

20-21—Moonrise over the Annapurna range

32-33—The Himalayas, Nepal

42-43—Everest colored by late-afternoon sunlight

52-53—Mount Everest and the Himalayan range from Pang-La
        Pass, Tibet

64-65—Pack ice in Beaufort Sea

74-75—Makalu landscape

92-93—Terraced mustard fields in Nepal

100-101—The Himalayas

110-111—Terraced rice fields

Picture Acknowledgments

AP/WIDE WORLD PHOTOS: 2, 26, 50 (top), 54, 55, 66 (bottom), 69, 70, 73, 94, 113

THE BETTMANN ARCHIVE: 36, 56, 117

©CAMERAMANN INTERNATIONAL, LTD.: 17, 96 (top), 99, 103; COURTESY ASAHI SHIMBUN, 14

THE MARILYN GARTMAN AGENCY: © FRANK A. SPOFFORD, 10–11; © BRENT WINEBRENNER, 30, 35, 50 (bottom), 52–53, 107

© VIRGINIA GRIMES: 24, 100–101

PHOTRI: 6–7, 66 (top); © M. FANTIN, 39

H. ARMSTRONG ROBERTS: © A. GEISSER, 19; © V. CLEVENGER, 27, 32–33, 34, 37; © K. SCHOLZ, 64–65; © G. ROESSLER, 95; © KOENE, 96 (bottom)

ROOT RESOURCES: © BARBARA ADAMS, 18; © W. HELFRICH, 72

SHOSTAL ASSOCIATES/SUPERSTOCK INTERNATIONAL, INC.: 63; © HERBERT LANKS, 57

TOM STACK & ASSOCIATES: © SPENCER SWANGER, 42–43, 48; © DAVE WATTS, 68; © GARY MILBURN, 104; © MANFRED GOTTSCHALK, 110–111

TONY STONE WORLDWIDE/CLICK-CHICAGO: © DAVID SUTHERLAND, 20–21, 31; © ANNE SAGER, 92–93

SUPERSTOCK INTERNATIONAL, INC.: 13, 71

UPI/BETTMANN NEWSPHOTOS: 4, 5, 9, 16, 23, 51, 59, 60, 61, 62, 67, 77, 98, 109, 115, 118, 119

VALAN: © MARTIN KUHNIGK, 15; © B. TEMPLEMAN, 25, 28, 29, 38, 40, 44, 47, 49, 58, 97

FROM *HIGH IN THE THIN COLD AIR.*

© 1962 FIELD ENTERPRISES EDUCATIONAL CORPORATION USE BY PERMISSION OF WORLD BOOK, INC.: 74–75, 76, 78, 79, 80, 81, 82 (2 photos), 83, 84, 87, 88, 90, 91, 116

COVER ILLUSTRATION BY STEVEN GASTON DOBSON

About the Author

Timothy Gaffney is a military affairs/aerospace writer for the Dayton *Daily News* in Ohio. His reporting has put him in the cockpits of some of the newest airplanes, including the B-1B bomber and the navy's F-18 fighter. His feature writing has included articles on whitewater raft trips, backpacking, and mountaineering. Mr. Gaffney has also written several children's books on the subjects of science, aviation, space, and exploration. He and his wife, Jean—whom he met on a backpacking trip—live in Miamisburg, Ohio, with their four children.